MY SPIRIT SANG ALL DAY

A Life in Music

By Elizabeth Werry

For Jane, Mary, James and John

My Spirit Sang All Day

My spirit sang all day
O my joy.
Nothing my tongue could say,
Only My joy!
My heart an echo caught
O my joy
And spake,
Tell me thy thought,
Hide not thy joy.
My eyes gan peer around,
O my joy
What beauty hast thou found?
Shew us thy joy.
My jealous ears grew whist;
O my joy
Music from heaven is't,
Sent for our joy?
She also came and heard;
O my joy,
What, said she, is this word?
What is thy joy?
And I replied,
O see, O my joy,
'Tis thee, I cried, 'tis thee:
Thou art my joy.

Robert Bridges (1844–1930)

Contents

Devon

My earliest memory is of a shady room looking onto a big sunny garden. This was Fairfield, a rambling old house at the top of Totnes, on the ancient Roman Road, and the occasion must have been a family tea party, probably on a Sunday afternoon. My little sister and I were sitting on tiny little chairs with painted wooden backs (mine was fawn, Diana's was orange) and we were some distance from the big table where my mother and father and paternal grandparents (Granny and Pater) were sitting with our big brother John. I vividly remember the brightly coloured china teapot, the red, green and white embroidered tablecloth, and the glass fruit bowl in an elaborate silver frame – all of which I saw again many years later and instantly recognised.

War was imminent, and this was most probably a family meeting, perhaps to make big decisions. My father was about to be called up to Liverpool to the Intelligence Corps. Into our idyllic surroundings we were destined to have five people billeted.

Of course, I knew nothing of this. I was about three at the time, my little sister one-and-a-half, and my brother seven. We had moved to Fairfield from Plymouth, so that John and I could go to school at Dartington, which at that time was run by the progressive couple Leonard and Dorothy Elmhirst. I remember little of my time at the Parsonage, save that it was very happy, and my brother liked it so much more than Plymouth College where, as a reserved and rather shy little boy, he had been bullied. Life at Fairfield, with a large Alsatian (Peter) and what seemed to me like a vast garden (where I'm told I played for hours alone among the vegetable patches, digging happily), was about to change. I remember standing up in my cot in the basement – probably scared by the air raid sirens, or perhaps woken by our dog howling: he was so disturbed by the bombers targeting the Plymouth dockyards that he had to go. Anyway, a decision was made. Take the children to Australia, my father said, the war will be over in two years. He and my mother went to the shipping office, only to be told, 'Sorry, no more ships to Australia. The last one was torpedoed last week, but you can go to Canada.' Canada! Who do we know there?

Our parents had met at university in Exeter (of which more anon). This was then known as the University College of the South-West, Exeter, and was part of London University. The campus then, as now, occupied a very beautiful part of the city. There were, in the '20s, no halls of residence for women, so although my father's college was Reid Hall, my mother and her girlfriends were accommodated at Sandford, a hostel in the charge of a fear-some lady, one Mrs Bottisham. Fortunately, one of my mother's friends, Rene (who had read English) had married a Canadian, Leslie, and it was arranged that we should cross the Atlantic somehow and go to them in Montreal. Communications in those far-off days cannot have been easy: people did not readily telephone, and trunk calls had to be booked. During the next few months, however, everything was packed up and put into storage in a distant Devon farmhouse – most of which never appeared again – and in August 1940, we all caught the train to Liverpool, to board the P&O liner, Duchess of Atholl, sailing away from England to Canada for an untold length of time.

I remember the night-time train journey to Liverpool, wearing my bright-blue dressing gown with the blue-and-white rope belt; my teeth were chattering with the cold, or perhaps with apprehension at leaving my adored father. I am told that on departing I said, 'When I shall see Daddy again, Daddy shall say, "Who is this fine lady?"' What a wrench it must have been for both parents, for my mother especially, taking three children, aged eight, four and two-and-a-half, into the unknown.

Our journey by sea was memorable for me because of an accident that happened early on in the voyage. Every few hours, it seemed we had a different drill, which of course entailed putting on huge lifebelts, cumbersome enough for adults, but well nigh impossible for small children to move around in. Somehow, I fell down a gangway, cutting my tongue rather badly – and have retained a deep scar all my life. I can remember the doctors in green, the attention from everyone, and even the pain of trying to eat. Quite a lesson for all of us.

The following extracts are from letters written most days by my mother, and sent back to my father, recounting our adventures on the long journey (2,770 mile voyage) from England and air raids to safety in Canada.

'I expect you are wondering how we are getting on. It's 8.15pm and they're still loading luggage. We had lunch at 2.15 – and what a meal it was! I'd forgotten how well they feed you on board ship.

"We had our first boat drill at 5.30, a terrifying noise of hooters and sirens. Then all the children, laden with enormous cork-filled lifebelts, had to climb to the top deck.

"There are 900 children on the ship, many of the little ones were at their last gasp, and there was a lot of weeping. But at 6.30 we had another sumptuous meal, which cheered us up. This is what we all had: Hors d'oeuvres, tomato soup, halibut, roast beef and vegetables, ice-cream, <u>and</u> an orange! Diana has found her spiritual home and is doing very nicely, thank you! John asked loudly if I had paid for all this feast, and when he had climbed with difficulty into his top bunk, he said he had never felt so full!"

The tugs took the ship out of the harbour and the voyage to the new world had started. Next day was not so happy.

"The sea was very rough. Elizabeth fell down, another kiddie, unable to see because of his big lifebelt, fell on top of her. Then Elizabeth was seasick. Only forty people in to dinner, and I wasn't one of them. Most people on board are very matey – a lot of dignity is lost when one is completely sick before a deckload of strangers."

The next day the escort left them, and the convoy split up.

"The two other ships that had been with us signalled to us with flashes. Then came noises like a distressed cow from our funnel, and the other two ships turned and went South.

"John has been enjoying himself all the time. I see him only for meals. But it is not such fun for the small children, nor is it for the mothers. Carrying them up to the top deck for boat drill, with their lifebelts on, and the rugs, is no joke. Sometimes I've felt hardly able to climb up myself, aware of constant danger from mine and submarine.

"Lying in my bunk feeling awful, I realised what superlative courage the early explorers had in their wretched little ships, so long at sea – with disgusting food and such overwhelming odds against them.

"We have taken a Northerly route, so for three days it has been exceedingly cold and impossible to stay on deck in the driving rain. We have had fog too. The children have needed their heaviest clothing, even leggings.

"Today, in the afternoon, everyone piled excitedly on deck to watch icebergs. We saw six, of which two were as wide as Fairfield, and the height of one storey. They were about 200 yards away from us. There was unfortunately no sun, but the sight was beautiful. The ice was streaked with lines where the next piece would break off, and showed the loveliest bright green as the water broke against its sides.

"At the same time we sighted land. How glad I shall be when this voyage is over! There are 1,300 people on this ship, and 900 of them are children. Naturally we have had few opportunities for amusements, the result being that idleness and boredom make the kiddies pester each other and all the rest of us.

"A great inconvenience has been the Western Time. Every night the clock has gone back an hour, and every morning the children have woken up an hour earlier! You ought to hear the din in the morning – it's bad enough all day. Our clocks are now five hours back, and we are nearly at the other side of the world. The Magnetic North is also affecting my watch with loses shockingly.

"Today has been utterly different. We awoke to brilliant sunshine, which kept on to a blazing sunset. Some passengers, including, of course, John, saw a whale spout. An enormous bird hovered over us and perched on the mast. Nobody could say if it was an albatross. It had a strange, sidelong flight, rather like a crab's movement.

"We should reach Quebec tomorrow morning, so I've sent you a cable which should reach you at about the same time. It will be very thrilling to be on dry land again and really on the move. The children are well. They have stayed up to 6.30 dinner most evenings, the reason being that the ices are larger than those given with the 5 o'clock tea!

"Well, I must end this long letter. We think and talk about you lots, especially me. I can picture you listening anxiously to the radio for news of shipping, just as we hang on the Overseas programmes.

"All the danger of the journey is now over. What a relief – no more lifebelts to lug about.

"All our love – be sure to look after yourself well."

Canada

Our voyage across the Atlantic lasted about eight days, and my mother describes in a letter home the final days on the ship as we sailed up the St Lawrence River towards our destination, Montreal:

"The scenery along the river St Lawrence is beautiful. Huge, uneven slopes – thickly wooded, with a few scattered houses. There are little churches everywhere, with very high, pointed spires.

"But during these last two days, when the scenery was really worth watching, we had to spend all too much time over formalities, queuing up for passports, baggage, doctors, tickets and so on. One had to rush all over the ship so as not to be late for the next queue. It was all very tiring for the children; the two little ones would never leave me.

"The noise on the ship had got on everybody's nerves, and nobody was sorry to say good-bye. We had breakfast at 6.30am and left the ship at 9. Through the Customs, and we were in Canada at last!"

Our friends in Montreal, Leslie and Rene, made us so welcome, and we stayed with them, I believe, for a couple of weeks, recovering from our sea journey. We children were wonderfully pampered, and Diana and I remember our first ever experience of a big funfair, when we screamed with terror and delight as we zoomed up and over and down on the huge switch-back with Uncle Monty, Leslie's brother. We also drove up to Mount Royal, and here we had a great view of the city of Montreal and of the distant hills in the United States.

My mother's first concern in the new country was obviously to find a job. No money could be sent out from England for at least two years, and when Rene and Leslie told us of an English friend of theirs in Edmonton, the capital of Alberta, who worked for the Social Credit Party in the Government Buildings, it was suggested that he might be prepared to help us. So with Rene's help, together with a large box of food, we embarked on the four-day cross-country train journey (Canadian National Railway) through all the provinces we later came to know well.

"We left Montreal at 9.15pm and once more had to put our watches back an hour. I could not sleep, but did better the next night when we slept head to foot. The children woke up before five each morning.

"You remember what a wet Sunday used to be like at home? Well, travelling with three children all this way by train is ten times worse! Space is so limited. There is a tiny observation car at the end of the train, so occasionally we walk down eleven coaches to break the monotony. When the train stops we get out to buy ice cream and milk. I started buying milk on the train and was charged 35c – practically 1s 6d per pint! So now I generally get it at station restaurants for 10 or 20c

"For the whole of the first day the scenery was the same, beautiful but monotonous – pine trees and lakes everywhere.

We had several glimpses of Lake Superior: it looked like a vast sea fringed with pines.

"We passed a number of Indian camps. They still had wigwams. The women are short and squat, wearing bright red blankets.

"After two days' travelling there came a sudden change. The pines disappeared and soon the land was as level as a tennis court. Black soil, occasionally sown with Indian corn or wheat, but often just wild prairie. And so through Manitoba and Saskatchewan all day, stopping at a few small towns. We had an hour at Winnipeg, so, leaving the little ones asleep, John and I went for a walk. We were glad to stretch our legs, but all we had time to see reminded us of Union Street, Plymouth! Until today we have had very cold weather, but now it has turned quite hot. This is no joke, as the windows on the train cannot be opened, and the sleepers get stifling at night. The porters on the train are all black, much to the children's entertainment. Through Alberta the scenery was very much the same, but as we neared Calgary, the land was less level. I noticed wheatfields everywhere and some cattle. At Calgary we had to change into a small local train, and the next seven hours were the worst part of our long journey. Fatigue and excitement combined to make the children infuriating. We reached Edmonton in the late afternoon, in the middle of a rainstorm which turned the roads into mud. But we were met at the station with a warm welcome which made up for a lot. The people here are very friendly and kind.

"Our two little ones have given me a lot of trouble. I think the high altitude has upset them, as well as all the travelling. It is a fearful job to get them to sleep, and during the day they will never leave me.

"John is getting spoilt. Ever since our train arrived, he has been treated incessantly to candies, ice-cream sodas and money! This afternoon he wandered away from us. After we had waited two hours for him, a radio call was sent out for him and we went to the police. At five o'clock John returned, knowing his way perfectly. He had made friends with an Edmonton lady who had spent the afternoon treating him!"

We were staying with Mr and Mrs Patrick Byrne, a very English couple, with a boy and a girl, and with four more mouths to feed, and all of us feeling by now more than a little homesick, we soon moved to rented accommodation and my mother began a job in the government buildings. She was broadcasting a correspondence course in French for listeners up North – I always believed it was designed for the trappers who lived up around Great Slave Lake, but this may not have been so. Somehow, my mother found a little clapboard wooden house for us in the West End of the city, a Ukrainian maid to care for us while she was at work, a little school locally for John, and a kindergarten for Diana and me. The news soon got round that there was an English family in the district, and the most heart-warming moment came on Christmas Eve, when a knock on the door revealed a group of local parents absolutely laden with everything we could have wished for – turkey, Christmas pudding, presents for us children, everything – they all seemed so delighted to be able to help the family from the "Old Country".

Although it must have been quite a struggle for a year or two, this was my mother's finest hour. Two years on she rented a bungalow in the University district on the South side of the great Saskatchewan River – crossing the High Level railway and road bridge – and we all started school at the Garneau Public School near our house (11054 – 83rd Avenue). I can still remember the phone number: 35205.

In the 1940s, Edmonton was a boom town. Oil and natural gas in abundance meant that things were burgeoning in all directions. With a first-class degree in French, my mother was appointed to a lectureship at the University, and life for her became less fraught. She still continued with her broadcast programmes, however, and this was no doubt to help finances. She hired a piano, and found an Austrian refugee teacher to visit the house every Tuesday after school to teach us. In April 1943, we went to a studio downtown and made a wax disc record to send to my father (now a Captain). This disc (very crackly now) contains our childish voices giggling and talking to him, acting a little scene (Mrs Tea Leaf and Mrs Curdle having tea together), John playing "Polly-Wolly-Doodle" on the piano, me playing "Little Fairy Waltz" (both hands, after only four lessons) and all of us talking together to him in broad Canadian accents about toys and books he had managed to send us: "Thank you for the gollywog, Daddy", a lovely Alpha Farnell monkey (always my mascot, even through university, where it was known as Euphrosyne), and some treasured books. Among these were all the A.A. Milne stories, from "When we were Very Young", "Now we are Six", through to "Winnie the Pooh" and "The House at Pooh Corner". These joined my favourites by Enid Blyton ("The Enchanted Wood" and "Mr Meddle's Mischief"), not forgetting the original orange-coloured hardback "Babar Story Book". Another interesting little story – an introduction to science – was "Droppy, Splash and Dew Pearl", and each of the raindrops was, of course, one of us. John was Droppy, I was Splash and Diana was Dew Pearl. We loved this distant connection with our remote father, who was now just a photograph on the wall – a British

Army Captain, in a soldier's uniform, with a severe-looking moustache. We all became great readers, and other favourites included "Girl of the Limberlost" (Gene Stratton Porter), the "Anne of Green Gables" series, "Little Women", and the books about "What Katy Did". We had occasional letters from my father – always on microfilmed paper in little brown envelopes – and I can remember laboriously writing him thank-you letters from time to time.

Canada was very keen to support the war effort, and we were encouraged at school to bring along any kind of lard in tins. I think this was to help in the manufacture of munitions. We were all very patriotic, and there was constant reference at school to the Old Country. Every morning in Assembly, we stood facing the Canadian flag, and solemnly declared:

> "I salute the flag, the emblem of my Country, and to her I pledge my love and loyalty."

Then we would all sing the National Anthem, "O Canada". All this before lessons began.

Elementary school in Canada began at the age of seven, so we could read and write before we began Grade 1. Most of this work I think must have been done at Kindergarten and with my mother, for we always had a lot of books in the house. I do not remember ever having any homework to do, but we were always reading, or playing the piano. Before school, we had a routine of a half-hour practice each between 7 and 8.30. The clock was on the top of the piano, and the schedule was rigidly adhered to, taking it in turns to be first, second or third. Then at half past eight, the three of us would walk the mile or so together up to school, the Garneau Public School.

Every district had an ice rink, and it was usual all through the winter after school to spend an hour or so skating at the rink before getting home. My brother John became a good ice hockey player, and Diana and I began to have figure skating lessons at the West End rink, which meant taking the street-car by ourselves over the High Level bridge there and back. One evening when I was about seven and a half, we were waiting for our lesson to begin, and started to play with the ice hockey sticks and a puck which had been left lying about. In the midst of our game I fell over and hurt my left wrist. Later that evening, after a late supper, the pain in my wrist got worse, and at about 10 o'clock I was taken to the University Hospital where an X-ray revealed a break. I went back to school next day with a plaster cast from my fingers to my elbow, and for six weeks everybody drew faces on it. We were taught to write listening to rhythmic music, and would practise a page of one letter at a time until our teacher (Miss Boss) was satisfied with it. I must have been in a rebellious phase at this time, for I remember being let off writing practice for quite a while so that my wrist could get better – but I always wrote with my right hand anyway, so there was some discrepancy there I fear.

Education in the province of Alberta was thought to be very good, compared with other provinces. We were well taught simple arithmetic, with great concentration on learning tables, and spelling bees were the order of the day. The geography of Canada was considered very important too, but I can remember seeing a map of the world after studying the Great Lakes and all the Canadian provinces. When I asked where England was, I was shown a tiny pink dot on the huge map – and could not believe that this was where we had come from, and where we really belonged. I think it was probably at that moment that I knew I wanted so much to go back to England.

But of course it was not possible. There were other British children in our school – including Sylvia Tait, from Sunderland, in John's class. She became a musician, like me, and we met years later at a Competitive Music Festival in County Durham. She returned alone to England by ship aged eleven. Then there was Carl Stansfield, in my class, who with his younger sister lived with an aunt near our school. Sadly his sister died in hospital of pneumonia, aged about six, much to the grief of their parents back in Wallington, and Carl was sent back to England as soon as it was possible. (I did keep in touch with him, and we exchanged visits while he was at prep school). Most of the time school was good fun; the holidays seemed long, and we led a very open-air life with few distractions.

One afternoon Diana and I were walking home down 83rd Avenue, and I recklessly decided to walk along the top of a brick wall. It was not very high, but I slipped and fell on my face, cutting my left cheek quite badly. Somehow we staggered home and Diana did her best to bandage my face till help arrived. Ping enlisted the help of our neighbour Irene, and we all went downtown to Mr Lobsinger the surgeon, who stitched me up with seven stitches, declaring that the scar would soon disappear. Despite my freckles, the scar has lasted all these years … Any upsets like this were usually helped by a visit to an ice cream parlour, where we would have an ice cream soda or a banana split.

Sometimes we would go for a long walk along the Saskatchewan River, and pick ripe saskatoons, which grew on large bushes, rather than near the ground like the much smaller blueberries growing in the Rockies. Sometimes we went horse riding from the stables of Biddy Greening, an eccentric English woman who had a huge dog named Poobah; but these excursions were rare.

At Halloween we would duck for apples floating in huge tubs of water. (They were always Kiwani apples from B.C. – I remember the crates, if not the spelling.)

As Diana's birthday was just before Christmas, we had a wonderful party for her one year (perhaps her seventh birthday). Ping hired a horse-drawn sleigh, and the driver took a whole crowd of us children around the snowy district, with sleighbells ringing, dashing past all the houses with Christmas trees in their gardens. It was just like "The Night Before Christmas", so exciting to be out in the dark, singing "Jingle Bells", and afterwards we came home for cocoa and, I think, marshmallows.

My main friends at this time were Denny Ryan, who lived across the road in an overheated, much smarter house than ours, and Lorie Hudson, who once gave me a little tapestry kit which said patriotically "There'll always be an England …" I also remember Aleda van Dusen, and Donna Whiteside (the daughter of an ENT surgeon). She and her family visited England after the war ended, and we did meet in London, but lost touch again later on. There were two very clever boys in my class – Malcolm Collins, who took up medicine and became Dean of the Dental School eventually, and Richard Dunlop who later studied in Europe. But sadly all these long-lost friends disappeared from view long ago.

Our little house was at the end of the block, so we had crossroads beside our small garden. The bungalow had three bedrooms, a sitting room, kitchen and bathroom, and a small verandah porch where we could eat during the summer. There was also a lobby at the back where we kept the ice-box. The milkman delivered our milk in large quart bottles with cardboard tops. In the winter the cream at the top would freeze and rise up out of the bottles.

Because Edmonton lies in the middle of a land mass, we had very cold winters and very hot summers. The house was centrally heated by ducted air from a boiler in the basement. During the winter months the snow was sometimes six feet high outside the front door, and we had to shovel away a path before we could get to the sidewalk. It was often twenty below zero for weeks at a time, and when the thaw eventually came, we used to stomp through the slush all the way to school in our galoshes and snow suits. One spring we all got measles, and had to have a quarantine notice stuck on the front door for the whole duration. As we three children got the infection one after the other, this went on for weeks. We then all had to have eye tests (having been made to wear dark-green eyeshades during our illness) and all of us had glasses thereafter. Needless to say, we didn't all wear them all the time – only Diana stuck to the rules.

About this time we had a studio photograph taken, to send back to my father in England, and I remember just as we were leaving the studio I was called back by the technician and asked if we wanted the freckles left in. I boldly answered for the lot of us and said, No, thank you. Too late to do anything about it later … I think it may have been that spring when I suddenly went down with pleurisy, and spent a week in the University hospital having mustard poultices applied to my chest. I also remember that the children's ward had polio sufferers in it, which at the time was common practice. The incidence of polio was very high, and if you didn't get it, it was assumed that you had got immunity through a bad cold. Well, we didn't seem to get colds much: Ping was an early health-food enthusiast. She cooked with olive oil and garlic (no doubt from having lived in France for a year in the '20s as a student), and made us eat wholemeal bread, raw carrots and celery, vegetables like beetroot tops and spinach, and plenty of liver, heart and tongue. I was a skinny little girl until we returned to England, and I was always under-weight at school, and allowed to have snacks between meals (Graham wafers with butter, I remember) – much to the chagrin of the others.

Our closest friends in Edmonton were Bill and Irene Austin, our neighbours in a big house across the road. Irene was a Hungarian aristocrat who lost most of her family during the war. She was a great support to all of us, and became Diana's godmother when she was christened at the new church of St John's, out beyond White Avenue in the ever-expanding Southside of the city. My mother also made several friends at the YWCA, including Ethel Hopkins and Nancy Thompson and her sister. These ladies were very kind to us children, and at Christmas-time we would be entertained to supper and given little presents. Nancy visited us later in England several times.

Other friends in the University were the Sonnet family (M. le docteur Sonnet was head of the French faculty) whose Sunday lunches were a special gastronomic experience; we looked for-ward to ice cream with wonderful toffee sauce. My only sad memory of Mme Sonnet was when she visited us unexpectedly one afternoon when Ping was making summer dresses for us, and we were being measured. She asked me to play something on the piano for Mme Sonnet, and as an awkward eight year old, I stu-pidly refused. I so much regretted that later after a mild reproof from my disappointed mama. Mary Faunt was another friend who later married Vic Graham, Professor of French in Toronto (whom John G.M. visited in 1980 with the King's Choir).

Another firm friend was Bill Innes, an elderly Scottish climber whom my mother met at the Alpine Club in Banff. He took us climbing up Sulphur Mountain on one of our camping trips

to Banff and Jasper. We camped around the lakes of the area
– Emerald and Moraine Lakes, Lake Louise (even had an icy-
cold dip there once) and once at Banff our tent was burgled,
when we were out, by some black bears attracted by the tins
of clover honey. Bill took us to walk over the Columbia ice-
field with Wendy, our dog. This must have been Spring in 1944.
I remember it was very cold, and after walking on the glacier
for a good long time, we got back in the car (a Ford V8) and
drove away down the snowy highway for a few miles before
suddenly realising Wendy was not with us. Bill turned the
car around and drove back, to find Wendy sitting motionless
alone in the middle of the road exactly where we had left her.
What a fright ...

But the summers in Canada were absolutely wonderful. When
school finished, we three would often walk down to an open-
air swimming pool (past a large smelly brewery and through a
wooded area on the banks of the Saskatchewan River) and spend
hours there. John and Diana became excellent swimmers and
divers; I never did. Sometimes, schoolfriends would have birthday parties in the woods, cooking hotdogs over an open fire, or
corn on the cob, and we usually had ice cream. Our dog, Wendy,
always seemed to be with us. Perhaps that is just my childish
memory, but this black/brown/white mongrel was our constant
companion, and always came on holidays with us when we went
camping in the Rockies, or to a house at the lake.

During August, Ping taught at the summer school in Banff, and
we children would spend weeks at Aberfeldy, an old wooden
house with wire mosquito netting over the windows, at Seba
Beach, about 60 miles south of Edmonton. It was not too far
from Banff, so although our maid Leona was in charge most of
the time, we all had weekends together.

We would shop at the little local store, and often bought an apple-and-raisin homemade pie. Another treat was an "all-day sucker" – a really big lollipop covered with chocolate. Sometimes at the lake we would have a taffy-pull in the kitchen. This meant slowly cooking a large pan of golden toffee on the wood-burning ancient old black stove, and then, when the toffee had nearly cooled, pulling the ends of it to see how far we could stretch it across the kitchen. We also loved to cook popcorn during the holidays.

Occasional thunderstorms added to the excitement of being away from our home in Edmonton, and one event was scary enough to assume great importance in our memories. There was a boathouse down on the lake run by an old man (Guy Stirling, I think was his name) who hired out boats for visitors. Most of the regulars had a little rowing boat and their own landing stage, as we did. One thundery evening, a group of off-duty servicemen came down for a spin on the lake, and went roaring off in a speedboat. Unfortunately, they got entangled in the reeds at the far end of the lake, which everyone avoided because it was not safe for swimming there. We children never quite knew what happened that evening, but we were aware, because of all the noise, that something was happening. The young men (possibly the worse for wear) had tried to swim, got stuck in the reeds, got cramp, and at least one drowned. Of course, this was a dreadful thing to happen, and we all grew up a little more.

As we became more aware, we gradually learned a little about our mother's family background. She was born Iris Mary Cobley, an only child, on 27 July 1907. Although she was born in a suburb of Liverpool, where her father was working at the time, her paternal family were seafarers from Brixham, South

Devon, and had been so for generations. Her father, Arthur Cuming Cobley, was a younger son of a sailing ship captain, who, together with his eldest son Thomas, was washed overboard at sea during a famously documented storm in the Bay of Biscay in 1867. Until then, as Commodore of a number of merchant ships, the family had led a very privileged life as highly respected members of the Brixham community.

We have an ancient bound copy of the New Testament in the family, given to my mother's grandmother (Elizabeth Cuming Swaffin) by *her* grandfather (John Cuming) in 1844. In his beautiful copperplate hand, the fly leaves of this bible contain a touching account of the cholera epidemic of the early 1830s, beginning apparently in India, and travelling all over Europe (presumably by ship) to Falmouth, where John Cuming was then living. He records the deaths of innumerable people of all classes.

Following the sudden death of both husband and eldest son in 1867, widow Elizabeth Cuming Swaffin Cobley had a struggle to bring up her surviving children: John, George, Elizabeth, Arthur, and the baby she was then carrying (subsequently also named Thomas). Their standard of living plummeted. The shipping company made no provision for the family, except that the boys were sent to a severe naval boarding school for the children of drowned Merchant Navy officers. My mother's father and his brothers had unhappy memories of this establishment. Education was severe but efficient. They wrote the usual copperplate hand, and, like all the family, read widely. But instead of being able to follow the Cuming/Cobley family tradition of working in small shipyards as sea captains and Trinity Pilots, they had to be content with jobs as clerks in shipping offices rather than anything more ambitious. My mother's father, Arthur, had such a post, as a commercial clerk in a shipping office importing and exporting coal, and moved about the country where the work was.

It was while he was working in Liverpool that Arthur met and married Gwladys Shaw, a young girl from the Lake District. Did he meet her in the church choir? Goodness knows – but despite the wide disparity between their ages (Arthur was in his mid-thirties, Gwladys fifteen years younger) my mother, Iris, was the result of this union. Gwladys' family came from Kendal, and we know that her mother was Mary Ellen, the rebellious older sister of Harriet Kendal, a quite well-known Edwardian singer, pianist and composer (1857–1933). The story goes that Mary Ellen was rowing on Lake Windermere one afternoon, when she, perhaps deliberately, lost one of her oars and was rescued by a dashing young red-haired Irishman by the name of Shaw. Was he an unfrocked priest? We don't know, but family legend has it that he wooed Mary Ellen, they eloped to the Continent with her money, did the Grand Tour and came back months later in time for her to give birth to her daughter, Gwladys, my mother's mother. This daughter grew up to become similarly adventurous and irresponsible, for soon after my mother's birth in July 1907, Gwladys disappeared abroad with a "cousin" in the import-export fruit business, leaving little Iris with her father. Divorce in 1910 or 11 was scandalous, and Arthur moved with his little daughter to London where he lived temporarily in East Ham with his brother John and sister Elizabeth (always known as Auntie Lizzie). Uncle John was by this time a Customs surveyor, prosperous, unmarried, having taken on the care of his aged mother and her sister who was bedridden.

Iris was sent to school at the age of seven (to a little primary school at the end of the road), but learnt to read, write and calculate at home with Uncle John. She had nothing but pleasant, happy memories of this time, with lots of lovely books about famous historical characters.

"Uncle was a good pianist, and I loved hearing him play when I was in bed.

"My mother and her new husband made one attempt to collect me when my aunt was out, but the maid would not let me go. Harriet Kendal offered to adopt me, but Pa refused.

HARRIET KENDALL (1857–1933)

Well-known as a contralto, composer, and pianist, Harriet Kendall grew up in the Lake District. She studied at the Royal Academy of Music, the Guildhall School of Music and King's College, London, and was taught singing by Manuel Garcia, who had trained Jenny Lind. Her dramatic and musical recitals at Queen's Hall, London, were very popular in their day. In these concerts she recited poetry, sometimes with her own piano accompaniment and occasionally with orchestral accompaniment. Based at her house 'Elsinore' in Twickenham, she played Shakespeare at various London theatres and was lecturer in elocution at King's College (Ladies' Department). *Synariss and Other Poems for Recitation* was published in London and New York. An obituary appeared in *The Times* following her death in an Eastbourne nursing home in September 1933. In her will, she endowed a Harriet Kendall Prize for elocution at the Royal Academy of Music.

"When the war came in 1914, like many people, we started to hoard supplies down in the basement in case of future shortages. There were broken nights with air attacks, although we were never hit, but it was decided that I should go to Cardiff where my father was now living and working in the Washed Coal Company – very successful until the War lost them their foreign markets later.

"So from 1917 I was back with my father, in a number of different lodgings, where I came across all sorts of people, and attended another state elementary school, from which I took the examination for higher education, and was 1st for the City of Cardiff.

"During the 5 years I was in Wales, I was close to my cousin Leslie, the son of my father's brother George. I attended Cardiff High School for Girls on a free scholarship, but we paid for all our books. These were expensive, as they changed constantly. But Pa never complained. Our uniform was black with red stripes, and we wore a cap with a peak. School was in a large old house, everything highly polished, and I loved it all. I don't think I worked hard, except at what I liked, but the opportunities were there. I was undisciplined, and took advantage of that.

"Every weekend I went with Pa to the cinema or theatre, and very early was introduced to many operas, as he loved them, and the Carl Rosa and Gilbert and Sullivan Touring Companies came regularly.

"Then at the end of the Autumn Term 1922, in the year when I should have taken the CWB (the Welsh GCSE), I suddenly had to leave school. Pa's job had gone; the firm went bankrupt, and we went back to the old house in Brixham. I went to Torquay Grammar School and took Cambridge Matric in the summer. Aunty and Uncle had in the meantime moved back from London to Brixham, where I had enjoyed summer holidays and always dreaded the return journey to Cardiff.

"So life was now easier, with Aunty Lizzie in charge; Devonshire food etc. With the necessary qualification, I decided to pass a year Student Teaching in Brixham for £12 a year."

During this year (1924) while Iris was also preparing for Higher Schools' Matric, she walked down the hill every morning to the primary school with a little boy called Bob Dart (later to become Thurston Dart, Professor of Music at Cambridge). From Brixham, Iris went to the University College of the South West,

Exeter, to read French. Much to the disappointment of her head-mistress at Torquay Grammar School the family were unable to afford the £200 p.a. for Oxford. At Exeter, Iris met her future husband, Roy James Werry – President of the Student Union – and they formed life-long friendships with historian W.G. Hoskins ("Uncle" William) and his cousin James (Canon Hoskins). For some reason, during her time at Exeter, Iris became known as "Ping" to her friends. We were never able to discover why – a few select buddies probably knew, but nobody would tell us the origin of this nickname, which stuck throughout her adult life. My father always called her Ping, and so did my brother John from his earliest years. To me and Diana in Canada she was always Mummy until we grew up. Then we all relapsed into Ping-mode, and of course later on she became Nanny Ping.

At college, Iris was the Belle of the Ball, an excellent tennis player and dancer, and did very little work. Too much partying, and she failed her degree! She went to France for a year and taught in Lyon. On returning to England, she took her degree again and got a First (B.A. Hons French). She was known to be "progressive" in her views, and after a year teaching at St Michael's School, Tavistock (while RJW was teaching Science at Blundell's) they eloped during the summer of 1931. Iris taught briefly at Bromley High School, but later that year they settled north of Plymouth in a house called "Tanglewood" (newly built), where John was born in May 1932 and Elizabeth in May 1936. When RJW began to teach Science at Devonport High School, they moved to Totnes, into a roomy old property, Fairfield, and acquired first a red setter (Chops), then an Alsatian (Peter), and, in December 1937, another daughter, Diana.

Of our father's family, we knew little until we returned to England in 1947. Only one of our grandparents remained alive

– Alice Beatrice Goff, my father's mother. She was born in 1872 and lived until January 1962 (her last three or four years spent with us in the family home in Cuffley, Hertfordshire). She had married my grandfather James Artemas Werry in 1904 but he died of TB when my father was nine. Widowed at around forty, my grandmother moved with her young son to the Goff family home on Salisbury Plain, Plymouth. Her older brother William (Uncle Will) had two boys, Bill and Reg, who with young Roy became inseparable companions. They were like brothers, led into innumerable scrapes by Bill, the adventurous eldest. Reg, the sensitive artist, became the Art master at Sittingbourne Grammar School for the whole of his career. He married Mildred, and they had one daughter, Christine, born with Hirschsprung's disease. As Christine was about the same age as Diana and me, we saw a good bit of her as teenagers. She was in and out of hospital for years, but eventually became a Queen Alexandra's nurse, married Lesley Drewe, and had one daughter. Bill Goff lived in Sheffield, where, in addition to many business interests, he ran a dairy farm at Dore. He had two children, Geoffrey and Geraldine. Geoffrey died of stomach cancer in 1986.

As a boy in Plymouth in the early years of the 20th Century, young Roy grew up with Bill and Reg, admiring them both. Uncle Will taught History at Devonport High School and illustrated his lessons graphically, often acting the stories hiding under classroom tables apparently. The boys all loved him. When she was widowed, his younger sister Alice (my grandmother), also a qualified teacher, went back into teaching at a school for handicapped children because the salaries were higher. Her own friends in Plymouth included the Foot family (especially Alice, the mother of Michael Foot M.P.), also Mary Waterman (sister-in-law), Annie Whitburn, Eva Marsh, Emily

Warren, Marion Bailey and H. Feldermann. Many of these young women were gifted water-colourists, and the autograph book my grandmother gave me in 1950 contains some lovely painting by Alice Foot (fuschias, 1903), a pastel of frogs dancing on toadstools by Maud E. Marsh (1903) and another of three cats by Ernestine Bird (1919), a watercolour of yachts by Donald Floyd, her cousin, and a lovely sketch (Head of Ullswater) by Reg Goff in 1918, when he was just eighteen. The book also contains a lovely watercolour of daffodils by my grandmother, Alice Goff (1903), a watercolour of red roses by Ada M. Whitburn (1903) and a drawing of cowslips by Marjorie Spendlove (1920). We have two attractive autumn scenes, watercolours (framed) by my grandmother. She also painted well in oils: James G.M. has a painting of Hastings harbour, and I have a windmill scene. By her cousin Donald Floyd RA. there are a number of Devon moorland scenes in the family's possession – Quantock hills (owned by Elizabeth), Tintern Abbey (owned by Diana), an excellent watercolour of boats, one named Annie, Donald's wife; also an oil painting of a country cottage in a Devon lane, owned by Jane R.M.

A few years later, my grandmother met her second husband through the church they both attended in Plymouth. He was Albert Edward Giles, a widower with two daughters, Phyllis and Doris. He was always known to us as "Pater", and was a kindly, dignified, Edwardian gentleman. Pater was an indulgent husband and a successful businessman, and encouraged my grandmother to buy whatever she pleased in the elegant post First World War shops of provincial Plymouth. His two rather plain daughters were several years older than their newly acquired stepbrother Roy, and it must have been galling for them to find him winning prizes and scholarships, while they struggled on having sadly lost their own mother. I have a clear memory of meeting Phyllis when I was about twelve, and she seemed to me then a rather sad, lonely spinster (aged about fifty-five) with a boring job she didn't enjoy, and a gloomy outlook on life. We went for a family walk on Dartmoor and she moaned constantly about the difficulty of walking down a little hill. I felt concerned for her, but also sad to think what a sorry kind of sister she must have been to my father when he was growing up. Her sister Doris married and had a son, Graham Rutherford, who read Maths at Queens' College, Cambridge, contemporary with me in the late 1950s.

Granny and Pater lived in Plymouth ("Caradon", Venn Crescent, Hartley) all their married lives, and seemed to me to lead a steady, uneventful but happy existence. Granny as a young woman had been a noted contralto, and sang many big oratorio parts ("Messiah", "Elijah", Stainer's "Crucifixion" and so on) as required, either in the Methodist chapel (where she brought up my father to godly learning) or in other local venues such as St Andrew's Church, Plymouth, where John and I were christened. My father was a very good boy treble, and sang such parts as the shepherd boy in Mendelssohn's "Elijah". When his voice broke, he sang a lot of Victorian ballads, and at College often entertained with the popular "Indian Love Lyrics" of Amy Woodforde-Finden. When we returned to England he would occasionally sing to us, but I am ashamed to admit that I did not appreciate what a good natural baritone he had. I remember disliking the jolly ballads he sang, and, with the ignorance and impatience of youth, I scorned songs about Drake and other Devon seafaring heroes.

We know relatively little of my father's family background. They were yeomen of the West Country, originally from Cornwall, and we have traced a William Werry (1726–1750), born in Duloe, died at St Blazey, a tin miner. He had two sons, and from one branch we found James Werry who married a Welsh woman, Mary Jenkins. They had five children, including twin boys. One of these was James Artemas Werry (died 1915), whose only son was my father, Roy James, born 1905 in Plymouth (died 1986). The other branch of the Werrys from St Blazey emigrated to South Australia in the 1830s and became sugar beet farmers. We know more about my paternal grandmother's family, the Goffs, also a West Country family. They, the Floyds, and the Watermans were a well-established artistic and musical family in Devon generations before my grandmother, Alice Beatrice Goff married James Artemas Werry in 1904.

Towards the end of our seven years in Canada, we all began to think about the next step in our lives – returning to the Old Country – war-torn, when we had had such protected lives away from it all. We spent two early summer holidays on Vancouver Island (British Columbia) in 1945 and 1946. We stayed at the Rosebank Auto Camp, not far from Victoria, living in raised wooden cabins high above a sandy beach, where we would spend the days swimming, digging for clams (which we would cook over the fire, and eat with butter) and enjoying many walks and picnics. It was lovely country and there were flowers everywhere. We met an English family, who had a small boy with a very English accent, and I talked to him a lot about life back in England. I think I imagined that we would soon be returning to an Edwardian lifestyle where the children lived in the nursery and saw their parents after tea. This had obviously come from my reading all those 1930s books ...

I remember one day at school, in Grade 3 I think, when Miss Boss was teaching us the old English folksong "The Oak and the Ash", and asked me to play it for the class. It was too difficult for me at that time – far too many flats (F minor) – and I was mortified that I could not do it properly. It is a very beautiful old tune with such evocative words, and I remember thinking of my Daddy so far away, and I felt sad.

My mother hoped that she might persuade my father to join us in Edmonton, where the job opportunities for a Science graduate were endless, and Englishmen were welcomed with open arms. But this never happened, and after the VE Day Parade on 9 May 1945 (which we watched from balconies down in the city) and some children returned overseas, we stayed on and our lives continued in much the same way. I had my tonsils out in Queen Alexandra's Hospital (lots of children did in those days), and at about that time I remember hearing about a girl we knew who broke her leg and her parents would not let her have it set because they were Christian Scientists. I never heard the eventual outcome of this horror, but I do remember the adults being up in arms over it.

I joined the Girl Guides, and also an organisation known as CGIT (Canadian Girls in Training), and I loved the uniforms (which I later brought back to England ...). I became a patrol leader in the Scarlet Pimpernel Patrol, and had a lovely time collecting badges to sew on my dark-blue uniform. The Scouting Movement was very strong in Canada, and John progressed up the ladder at a great rate – in fact, becoming a King's Scout shortly after we returned to England.

But that was not to be until June 1947, and after living for such a large part of our childhood in Canada, it meant leaving a lot behind. By this time, my father was demobbed and had been appointed to a Science Lectureship at an Emergency Training College set up by the Government to assist ex-servicemen to complete their degrees. This College was five miles from Preston in Lancashire, in a little mill town called Bamber Bridge (8,000 people in those days) and what my mother thought of this prospect we never knew.

Back in Edmonton, I was in Grade 4, Diana was in Grade 3, and John was in Grade 8, just beginning French at the age of fourteen. Our music was going well. John was playing big pieces like the Pathetique Sonata (Beethoven), I was into the Bach Inventions, and Diana was already at eight thinking she'd like to be a doctor, dissecting chickens on the kitchen table, and reading Dickens.

When we first began our piano lessons in 1943 with Paul Richel, an Austrian refugee, we played easy classics from a huge book called "Bach, Beethoven and Brahms". This book had literally hundreds of pages, and included easy arrangements of well-known melodies – anything from Beethoven's violin concerto to Brahms's Lullaby. There were also excerptsfrom the Bach English and French Suites, and I learned my first ever Bach Minuet (in B minor) from this book. It took me a fortnight to understand how the two parts fitted together. Then I found Sibelius's "Finlandia", and John learned a version of "Rustle of Spring" (Sinding) in A minor. This seemed a very hard piece to me; but many years later I realised it is really in the key of B flat minor – much more difficult. Thus we progressed to the two volumes of Kuhlau Sonatinas, mostly with three movements each. We each had our own particular sonatinas (and of all of them, I thought the A major was the best one). Whenever I hear one of these pieces now, they recall unmistakably those wonderful carefree childhood days in Edmonton. As we progressed, I used to remember page numbers, and learn John's pieces as quickly as he did. We all became good sightreaders, and although we were taught in a totally unstructured way, without any Scales,

Arpeggios or Theory, we had acquired a wide repertoire of interesting pieces when the time came for us to leave Canada.

My mother, planning our return to England, had to sell the contents of our little house, because we could take very little home. We were each allowed to take a very few books and treasures with us, and difficult choices had to be made. The hardest was the decision to leave Wendy, our much-loved dog. We eventually gave her to a lovely University family, the Andersons, who loved her and looked after her until she sadly died of a tumour a year after we left Edmonton.

That last year in Canada I went to my first-ever classical music concert. It was held in Edmonton's biggest concert hall, and made an indelible impression on me. I can even now remember that it was the Handel E major violin sonata, played by Isaac Stern and his Trio, which got me completely hooked. My mother took me there for the first half of the concert, and I then caught the streetcar home when John arrived for the second half. My head was spinning all the way home.

My only other memory of an evening's music was a performance of "The Gondoliers" (Gilbert and Sullivan) at the University, and this was probably an undergraduate production. I found the music unmemorable, apart from the chorus "Drink water, drink water, drink!", and my abiding memory is of a bright-blue backcloth to the stage – presumably the sky in Venice?

I remember taking part in a piano competition in the city concert hall round about my eleventh birthday. I played two set pieces – a little Mozart Sonatina in C, and a lullaby entitled "The Drone's Slumber" (by Helene Diedrichs). This was my first foray into the world of competitions, and I know I played the Mozart far too fast, messing up my chances of winning the class. Afterwards, however, a well-known pianist came up and asked my mother if she could teach me. It must have given Ping some comfort to be able to say, "So sorry: thank you very much, but we're going to England next week …"

And so we did: back the same way we came, four days on the train to Montreal. Of course, we were all seven years older, excited about returning to England and seeing our (pretty well unknown) father again. But the urgent need was for the three of us to learn Pounds, Shillings and Pence (11-plus was looming for me). So we all had a crash course in £ sh d. All we knew was decimals. When we got to Montreal, we were met again by our old friends – and of course they had to take us to the fairground again! You must enjoy yourselves now, they said, food and rationing in England will be terrible. And it was.

Fairfield, Totnes

Iris Mary Cobley,
1908, aged 6 months

Roy James Werry,
1908, aged 2

Iris, 1911, aged 4

James Artemas Werry, Alice
and Roy, 1913

Roy and Alice Werry, 1914

Iris, 1918, aged 11

Arthur Cuming Cobley,
1918

Reg and Bill Goff, and Roy, 1925

Iris, 1926, aged 19

Roy James Werry, BSc, 1927

Iris, 1928, aged 21

Ella Pounder, 1930

John, Diana and Elizabeth, 1940

Elizabeth Jane Werry,
1938, aged 2

Elizabeth, passport photo, 1940

Arthur Cobley, 1940

Elizabeth, 1942, aged 6

Capt. R.J. Werry, Intelligence
Corps, 1942

Govt. Bldgs, Edmonton, across
Saskatchewan River

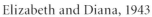

Elizabeth and Wendy, 1944

Elizabeth and Diana, 1943

John/Michael, 1944

Elizabeth/Jane, 1944

Diana/Mary, 1944

Elizabeth, John and Diana, Cowichan Bay, B.C., 1945

Elizabeth outside 11054 – 83rd Ave, 1946

John, Elizabeth and Diana, Saltburn-by-the-Sea, 1948

Lancashire

We left Montreal on June 25, 1947, on a BOAC Strato-cruiser bound for Gander (Labrador) and then Prestwick (Scotland). It was certainly a wonderful experience for us children. We had not been on a 'plane before, and everything was new. (The only disappointment was that they had run out of barley sugar, but I remember we had all been given one of the new biro pens that had just appeared – a present from Bill Innes before we left – and had fun writing with them.) Flying over England was a sight I'll never forget: it was like seeing a miniature farmyard with different-coloured fields all neatly marked off. We were used to seeing miles and miles of yellow prairie provinces with only an occasional grain silo to break the monotony of the flat fields. And the rain! We arrived at Prestwick in wet, wet weather, and had to find an LMS steam train to take us down to Preston where we would be met. En route, we had lunch on the train – I remember Brown Windsor soup and sausages – a typical welcome to post-war British food. Accompanied by the unforgettable smell of an old steam train.

We eventually got to Preston Station late in the afternoon. My father met us, dressed, I remember, in his white college blazer, and drove us back to the Training College at Bamber Bridge in a shooting brake borrowed from one of the other lecturers. We children must have been tired but very excited, and I recall sitting in the back seat working out how much pocket money I was owed, converted from Canadian dollars and cents into English money. When I ventured to say, "Daddy, I think you owe me a crown and fivepence," he laughed as if this was a very funny joke. Of course, I felt abashed and very silly: not a good start.

On arrival at our little prefab in the College grounds, however, we realised that a welcome party had been laid on for us by all the other families. Warned in advance that everyone had chipped in with precious rations to make cakes, jellies, biscuits and so on, we really did our best to be appreciative. But dried egg was strange to us, and difficult to enjoy, and the pink blancmange was absolutely horrible. The other children kept on saying "FHB" to each other, they were so thrilled to see such party food. We didn't know then the expression "family hold back" – in fact, the whole event passed in rather a blur. Certainly a major culture shock for us, and we must have been exhausted when we finally fell into bed.

Next morning, however, bright and early, we wanted to explore our new surroundings, and in the sitting-room I immediately discovered the upright piano. My father asked me to play something, and I now sat down and started to play one of the Bach Inventions I was playing at the time, no.1 in C major. The R.H. begins CDEFDEC G – and I stopped: "This piano is rubbish," I remember saying. "That's not C!" "What do you mean?" my father said. "I paid eleven pounds for that piano." "Well, anyone knows that's not C," I replied. The piano went back that day, and another one (with correct A440 pitch) arrived. It was the first intimation I had of having the mixed blessing of perfect pitch, and also began to realise that not everyone associates keys and letters with colours and characters. Musicians do not always have identical associations with keys. For instance, to me F#

major is "velvety", B♭ major is like water; B minor is a "windy" key. Some keys are very clear-cut, such as F major, which to me is a hard, bright sound; E major is very warm; D minor is desolate. These, and others, have always remained the same for me, and the colours of letters and numbers have not changed since I was a child.

Bamber Bridge Training College was built on an empty site beside the railway line, at the end of Mounsey Road, a wretched street of poor, brick, terraced houses opposite the cotton mill. On one side of the College there was a row of three-bedroomed staff bungalows, ugly prefabs. Other buildings included common rooms, lecture rooms, labs and student accommodation, and at the far end was a very large field where we would later on occasionally camp out at night, and watch the trains flying past all lit up.

The College was quite a convivial community, and we became friendly with the Spencer family next door, who had three daughters: Jean, Marie and Eileen (who became our special friend). We used to ride our bikes around the College towards a roundabout known as Piccadilly Circus, and sometimes played table tennis in the students' hall. There was also a tiny chapel, and at Christmas I recall the locals singing, "Earth was hard as eye-ron ..." etc, in the Lancashire way. We were, of course, trying very hard to lose our Canadian accents, and not pick up the local version.

As a very little girl, I was known as "Girlie" by my brother John, though this later on became "Skinny Lizzie". He was known at school as "Ginger" or "Werry, Werry, red as a cherry". As for Diana, she was always "Dinah" until she was about nine years old.

In Edmonton, we played Pick up Sticks, Chinese Chequers and, of course, Snakes and Ladders and Ludo, but there was not a great variety of board games for children around at this time. I don't remember that we had Monopoly until we returned to England.

Then, whenever we had a Christmas party, we would have a wonderful quiz of some sort, devised by father, who loved preparing such things. We also played Charades, and spent a good deal of time over meals discussing the meanings of words and phrases. He would regale us with Latin mnemonics that he had learned at Devonport High School as a boy, and never forgotten. Eg. "Caesar had some jam for tea" (*Caesar adsum iam forte*).

The summer we returned to England was a hot one by English standards. We learned that the winter months of 1947 had been extremely cold, and the hardships of post-war rationing soon became familiar to us. We did have blackcurrant purée, out of tins, every morning, and sometimes rosehip syrup, which we found repulsive. But food seemed very uninteresting, and without much variety. There was so little meat available I remember trying to like tripe, and another dish I found difficult to enjoy was cheese and onion pie. We did, however, take a shine to corned beef – probably because we hadn't had it during the war, so it was a novelty. The main street in Bamber Bridge had a butcher's shop (Mr Wolstencroft's) where we would buy the paltry amount of meat available to us on our rationbooks. It seemed that everything was in short supply, even bread.

Sometimes we would visit the dairy across the railway line that cut through the High Street. As well as selling milk, Mrs Miller also sold sweets in those lovely big glass jars with black lids. A quarter of mint imperials or pear drops would use a lot of our precious sweets coupons, but Diana, ever the sweetest of all of us children, sometimes went down to the shop on her own to pay the milk bill. "How's the baby today, Mrs Miller?" she would enquire, and after a few minutes chat would add "Got any sweets off points?" She was a most valued asset in those sugarless days.

There was also an ice-cream shop where they sold Milton's ices (blocks with wafers) and these seemed to us, after Canadian ice-cream, decidedly watery. But we got used to it, as we did to the local children marching up and down Mounsey Road in their clogs.

I sat the 11-plus exam in the County Offices in Preston that summer holiday, and passed well enough to go to Balshaw's Grammar School, a co-ed grammar in Leyland, founded in 1782. I would walk from the College in my new uniform (navy box-pleat tunic and white blouse and black and silver tie) down Mounsey Road to the bus stop at the end, running the gauntlet of the local women chatting on the doorsteps in their curlers and slippers. One morning as I passed two friends gossiping, I overheard one say: "I'm busting to go tu't lavvy ..." and she disappeared inside. Of course I repeated this later at home, and it became a family saying thereafter.

This was the year that the railways were nationalised, and suddenly the LMS uniforms disappeared, and on our little station (with the gates at the level crossing closing slowly whenever the bell rang) the railwaymen suddenly appeared in black and red, with BR on everything.

I spent four terms at Balshaw's, and made one very good friend, Ann Morris (later married to Canadian Jack Lewis) who became a penfriend when I changed schools, and remained a good friend through thick and thin over the years. I started at Balshaw's in Ic, the very bottom of the school, progressing to IIb for my last term. I remember particularly the teaching of English, my best subject at the time. The teacher was Miss Doherty (form mistress of Ic) and we read "The Water Babies" (Charles Kingsley). They would make me read aloud, and the class would snigger at my accent (especially the boys). I was upset when, although I was top in this subject, the comment on my report was "Elizabeth must guard against over-confidence". If it did anything, this remark made me even more self-conscious about my funny accent, and trying to speak English properly without adopting the Lancashire accent proved difficult.

Our classroom was in a prefab, heated by a stove at the back of the class, on which we would roast chestnuts – which sometimes exploded loudly. School dinners at Balshaw's were quite an experience: meat and two veg, and a pudding, all for sixpence. After my first term, the cost went up from 6d to 7d a day. We also had a little bottle of milk at morning break.

The school had the House system, and we were encouraged to be competitive in all sports. Not much success with me though. I remember standing on the pitch for hours in the cold, watching teams play hockey or football. But as I was only a very junior girl, I never got an opportunity to do anything much in the school, and was quite glad to leave at Christmas 1948, just after Prince Charles was born in November that year.

While we were in Bamber Bridge, Diana spent a year at primary school at Lostock Hall, where, because of her glasses, they called her "Speccy Four Eyes". Then she moved to Whittle-le-Woods, where the standards were much higher. John took his School Certificate at Preston Grammar School for Boys in 1948, where, against considerable odds, he managed to do well in his fifth form year with a lot of help from father. I remember seeing "Thank you, Dad," on his maths homework a few times. Diana and I had a few piano lessons from an inexperienced teacher (Alan Hitchen, trained at the Royal Northern College, Manchester), but I did not warm to him. At Balshaw's, we used the National Song Book, a red hardback book, which contained hundreds of well-known songs from all over the British Isles. We sang things like "The Bluebells of Scotland", "Early One Morning", "Farewell, Manchester", "When Irish Eyes are Smiling", "My Love's an Arbutus", "David of the White Rock", "The Ash Grove", and scores of others. This collection was widely used in secondary schools all over the country at the time, and it appeared in our next school, across the Pennines into the North Riding of Yorkshire. The music teacher was a very tall man, Mr Wilkinson.

With our friend next door, Eileen Spencer, Diana and I formed The Explorers' Nature Club, and this proved to be an exciting way to enlarge our knowledge of plants, insects and birds. We would take our bikes, sandwiches and a bottle of Tizer on the train down the line to Walton-le-Dale, or Cherry Tree, and collect specimens for the lab at the Training College from the nearby canal. Every visit we would write up in our diary, and the incentive was that we got paid by the Science lecturer (our father) for water boatmen, beetles, little water scorpions and other creatures needed in the labs. We also kept trifcnestrata in little cardboard boxes under our beds, waiting for fat green caterpillars to become cocoons, and eventually turn into lovely butterflies with the three windows on their wings. If I had been a scientist at heart, I could really have gone places. We had every opportunity. As it was, I just enjoyed writing up our adventures, doing a few drawings, watching the tadpoles in our little aquarium turn into frogs, and sticking photographs into my diary.

I also used to write stories at this time, very reminiscent of Enid Blyton's Adventure series. My brother John illustrated one of these for me, about some children who went off camping with a caravan and a dog called Rags. It wasn't a very good story, but later on I was to have more encouragement to write.

My father got his first Headship, of a small co-ed Secondary Modern School at the foot of the Cleveland Hills in the North Riding of Yorkshire. We crossed the Pennines and this was the start of another adventure for us.

Yorkshire

My father's new school was Redcar Lane County Secondary Modern School, and we moved into a terraced house near the seafront (50 Oak Road, Redcar). While the family moved across the Pennines, I spent a week in Wallington, Surrey, with Carl Stansfield (back from Canada) and his family. He now had a new brother, Jon, aged four. The Stansfields lived comfortably, and I enjoyed my time away, experiencing a different kind of life from the North. They took me up to London to the circus, and I began to get big ideas. Carl stayed with us in Yorkshire the following summer when he was preparing for Common Entrance. Later on, when he was at Repton, the family moved to a grand house in Ware (Hertfordshire) and Diana and I stayed there for an unforgettable summer in 1952.

Redcar Lane School was full of farmers' children, and very soon there was a flourishing Young Farmers' Club. We used to walk at the weekends up into the Cleveland Hills with our little black and white terrier, Junior, and one of our favourite spots was Upleatham Church, a tiny Saxon building, reputedly the smallest parish church in England. We also loved walking from Great Ayton over the fields up to Rosebery Topping, where the Captain Cook monument stands, commemorating his birth in the village below. One day our dog frightened some sheep and the irate farmer came roaring after us. Father calmed him down eventually, and the dog went back on the lead.

Redcar is a seaside town, which in the summer filled up with holidaymakers intent on ice-cream and Redcar rock. It boasts a very good old, established boys' boarding school (Coatham, Sir William Turner's Grammar School) which John attended in the Lower Sixth. However, the pressures of sixth form academic life did not suit him after the freedom and slower pace of Canadian education, and his interest in swimming and diving led him to excel in Outward Bound courses in Wales. He decided to join the Merchant Navy at the age of seventeen and a half. In this he was encouraged by both mother and father, who realised the sea was in his blood. He joined the John Holt Shipping Line, which ran merchant ships from Liverpool down to the West African coast, and John would be away for three months at a time. Then he would have a month at home to study for his Mate's Certificate.

My father became Chairman of Redcar Arts Guild, and we were lucky to have a steady stream of excellent chamber musicians in the concert series. Occasionally we entertained the artists at home for dinner before the concerts. There were also regular opera performances on film (a black-and-white Rossini "Barber of Seville") and I remember a very realistic and quite frightening colour film of Hieronymous Bosch paintings. We were friendly with Mr Willis, the headmaster of Sir William Turner's School, and his family. They lived in a huge schoolhouse (Red Barns), and had wonderful parties at Christmas, when we played all manner of hiding games all over the house – very exciting for us to have another four children, aged five to nineteen, to play with. The two girls in the middle were away at school in York; their big brother was at Cambridge. All this fired my enthusiasm for Angela Brazil books about boarding school life, and Elinor M. Brent-Dyer's "Chalet School" stories enthralled me.

Diana and I were now at the Girls' High School in Saltburn, and we moved there to a house off the Promenade (22 Emerald Street). Saltburn-by-the-Sea was to be our home for the next four years. The first winter we were there we were at Red Lodge, the lower school, an old Victorian mansion on the seafront. The North Sea thundered below the school, and we played hockey on the wide, hard sandy beach where sea coal was washed up on the high tide. Saltburn is dominated by Huntcliff, and there are wonderful cliff walks all along the coastal path towards Robin Hood's Bay, Staithes and Whitby. These are lovely little towns in the summer, but the North-East coast is constantly buffeted by cold winds during the winter months. A rift valley with a high road bridge lies at one end of the town, and there are beautiful gardens beneath, with an enormous monkey puzzle tree dating from Victorian days, when the town was developed with its Spa Hotel.

When we lived there between December 1948 and July 1952, Saltburn was a quiet little town, not much going on, mostly older people comfortably off, not many young families; only one school and a large Victorian parish church. The railway line (a branch line from Darlington) stopped at Saltburn, so it was a bit of a dead-end place. There was a Dr Barnado's home for girls nearby, a "nice" little private school ("The Towers") and a funicular railway to take people up and down to the beach, to save them the 200 steps.

Saltburn High School was noted more for its sport than for its academic prowess, though it did boast one illustrious old girl: Dame Kitty Anderson, Headmistress of North London Collegiate School. In the 1950s, a few girls aspired to university (Leeds, Nottingham, Durham), some went to training colleges, and very occasionally medical school.

At the beginning and end of each term, the Headmistress, Miss M.A. Bailey (known, of course, as Ma Bailey) would read this passage from Romans Chapter 12, verses 1–5, which became very familiar to us:

> "I beseech you therefore, brethren, by the mercies of God, that ye present your bodies a living sacrifice, holy, acceptable unto God, which is your reasonable service.

> "And be ye not conformed to this world: but be ye transformed by the renewing of your mind, that ye may prove what is that good, and acceptable, and perfect, will of God.

> "For I say, through the peace given unto me, to every man that is among you, not to think of himself more highly than he ought to think, but to think soberly, according as God hath dealt to every man the measure of faith.

> "For as we have many members in one body, and all members have not the same office;

> "So we, being many, are one body in Christ, and every one members one of another."

Of course, this was our school motto – "Members One of Another". Our school hymn was "To be a Pilgrim", and our school crest was the White Rose of York. In my Upper Fourth year, I was given a "Green Girdle", awarded for good deportment(!) and generally making oneself useful – in my case, playing the piano for Prayers, when Dickie Dyer, the music mistress, was indisposed. In my Lower Fifth year, during the external examinations when the senior girls were occupied, I was made a temporary prefect for half a term. Then a new Head arrived.

Miss Margaret Ellis arrived from Enfield Grammar School, and things began to look up. We had a flourishing school magazine, and were encouraged to write poems and articles for the magazine trophy, which I won in my Lower Fifth year, by writing an "Ode to a Prefect", a sonnet "To a Maths Mistress" (after Keats, of course) and an article called "A Canadian Winter". They all appeared in the 1951 School Magazine.

That year (1951) we performed Shaw's play "St Joan". I understudied for the main part (which was played by a girl in my form, Jean Ross), and I played D'Estivet, the Prosecutor. For this I wore my father's BSc hood and gown. The following year this play was one of our set works for English Literature "O" level (the new GCE exams had started the previous year). That summer I remember the speaker on Speech Day was the ballerina, Beryl Grey. She was lovely to look at, but I can't remember anything she said.

We like to remember Saltburn in the summer, when it was at its best, and we could enjoy swimming and lazing on the beach, expecially when John was home on leave. But for most of the year, this was a windy corner of the North Riding, and though we were intent on school things, there was not a lot going on there otherwise. There was, however, a flourishing rep. theatre company, and we saw many plays, some of which subsequently found their way South. Many of the less common plays of Shaw were performed here, and others I can't now remember.

Canadian Winter

The traditional Christmas of Dickens seems to have left this country forever, but in Canada, the white Christmas is an annual occurrence.

Almost every house has a large or small Christmas tree which stands in the front window, with the coloured lights turned on about four o'clock, when it gets dark. On Christmas Eve we used to walk (or rather slide) up and down the avenues, admiring the lighted-up trees that were growing in the neighbours' gardens, and bringing home not holly, but waving branches of evergreens.

One December night, a friend took us in a large party for a sleigh ride in the snowy country. We tied our toboggans and sledges behind the horse-drawn sleigh; and with much hilarious singing of "Jingle Bells," we set off along the dangerously hard, icy roads, which were as smooth as glass.

It is not an uncommon thing in Canada to hear during the late evening the sound of the sleigh bells and the laughter of the merrymakers out for a ride, mingling with the cries of those who have fallen off and have to run to catch up. But these unfortunates have nothing to fear from the snow, because everyone wears ski-suits, moccasins or ski-boots, and earmuffs when outside.

The coldest winter I remember was when it was fifty-four degrees below zero, and the snow was six feet high. But this did not trouble us, for we missed a few days school, although it was noon before we shovelled our way to the front gate.

At Christmas time all the schools have class parties in their own rooms. The pupils bring the food and the parties are held during school-time with the home teachers.

The greatest joy of winter to the Canadian child is, of course, ice skating. The rinks, scattered across the city, are free to every school-child from four until six o'clock on weekdays. Skating sometimes continues right up to the end of March. How we used to hurry out of school to change into our skates and rush on to the ice! There we used to practise figures in preparation for the Annual Carnival. This was held in the Edmonton Arena, a huge artificial ice rink which was generally used for ice hockey matches, and where the five thousand spectators would cheer the winning team to victory.

So ends a Canadian winter, full of sport, cheerfulness and vivacity; and just when one is wishing the ice would not melt so quickly, along comes a Canadian summer, and we quickly discard snow-suits and wind-breakers for sun-suits and straw hats, to keep us cool in the blazing sunshine.

Elizabeth Werry, Lower V (1).

ODE: TO A PREFECT

(With apologies to Keats' "Ode to Autumn".)

Damsel of power and utter ruthlessness!
Close bosom-friend of the maturing staff;
Conspiring with them how to load with ex-
Tra prep, the girls that in the classrooms laugh;
To bend always with toil their feeble frames
And fill all hearts with sadness to the core.
Till, in a wailful choir, the Fourth years cry
That "prees" must be abolished – and just why?
Because we think that life shall never cease –
Their "impots." have o'er-brimmed our prison cells.
"Where are my hockey pads?" "Ay, where are they?"
"Think not of them, thou hast thy lines to do."
So on an inky page, with patient look,
We write the final essay, hours by hours,
While barred windows hide the match from view.
And sometimes, like a teacher, thou dost keep
Steady thy learned head within a book,
Thy heart uplifted by the famous words
Of Keat's "Ode to Autumn" – till the bell
Awakes the stubborn prefect – and fare well!

Elizabeth Werry, Lower V (1).

Sonnet to a Maths Mistress

Oh! Giver of the Albegraic sighs!
How canst thou be so kind and yet so cruel?
That I should have to sit upon my stool,
While multiplying "x" and solving "y's";
That I should have to write terrific lies
To find "x", which is stubborn as a mule,
And thinking all the time, "Oh, what a fool!"
(A fool who on the morrow surely dies).
I'd make old Euclid hide his hoary face
To see my geometrical disgrace.
Pythagoras would turn his head in shame
If he beheld the misuse of his name;
But I must try my Algebra again,
Although these Maths. Are driving me insane!

Elizabeth Werry, Lower V (1).

The nearest big town was, of course, Middlesbrough, and we were fortunate enough to discover an outstanding piano teacher, Ella Pounder, who was very well known in the North East, and highly respected as a performer and teacher. She and the famous pianist Cyril Smith had both come from the same teacher in Darlington, and when Cyril became internationally known, Ella decided (after studying with the great Solomon) to return home from the R.A.M., marry Robert Clapham (a chemist from Billingham, who became a millionaire) and devote her life to teaching. She took on Diana and me, and I began (at twelve-and-a-half) a strict regime of slow practice. I still have my Bach Inventions copy on which she wrote, in her strong, unmistakable hand: "Try to play everything at a slow, steady pace." (This for no. 8 in F major, which is a fast piece, and well-nigh impossible to play well unless you have learnt it slowly.) Everything she taught me, in my twice-weekly lessons, became the basis of my own teaching later on. For me, she was the most inspirational teacher, feared by many of her pupils, but as I discovered later on, well-recognised in London for her pupils' successes in exams and competitions around the country. She sent many students to the Royal Academy on Open Scholarships, and during the four years I was with her, I competed in festivals all over the area, as far north as Newcastle, and down to London, winning trophies, cups and medals.

In March 1951 I won a Gold Medal for achieving the highest mark in the country (141/150) for Grade 6 Piano. Instead of a medal, I chose to have three bound volumes of the thirty-two Beethoven Sonatas, which have been in constant use ever since. Ella held a Theory class on Saturday mornings, and for someone who had no knowledge whatever of the principles involved, I had to struggle for a while before I got the hang of it. We all did one exam after another, one festival after another, and played in many concerts for her, and not just solos. We had duet partners, and on at least one occasion, four of us played on two pianos an arrangement of "Schwanda the Bagpiper" by Weinberger. This way we gained a huge repertoire, and were always encouraged to learn pieces from memory. Diana and I won Duet classes at local festivals – Eston, Stockton, Middlesbrough, to name a few.

One Spring (April 1952), just before I took GCE, I stayed in Ella's house for three days for intensive tuition and practice on the pieces I was preparing for an Associated Board Open Scholarship – the Beethoven Sonata in E flat, Op.7, and the Chopin Barcarolle, Op.60. In the event, I got through to the third day (into the final 6 out of 120) of the Competition, held at the Royal College of Music in South Kensington, but did not get one of the two scholarships awarded that year. I was given a County Major Scholarship by Yorkshire to study at the R.A.M., but decided to go to school in London when we moved South that summer.

I was in the Upper Fifth that year at Saltburn High School, in the "A" form. There was no streaming in different subjects in the school, so I had a hard time in maths (couldn't really under-stand calculus and trigonometry), so ended up doing maths at home with my father, and having some free time at school. Somehow I scraped through: we sat Northern Universities joint Matriculation Board where the standard was probably not very high. One of the subjects I most enjoyed (and we all did about ten subjects) was English, and our set works for "O"level included "Pride and Prejudice" (Austen), Keats' Odes, and "The Tempest" (Shakespeare). A wonderful treat that Easter was a visit with Ping to Stratford to see this play, with Margaret Leighton as Ariel, and Robert Helpmann as Caliban – unforgettable: wonderful dancer, but incredibly ugly.

We played cricket in the summer, on playing fields beside the school. We lived about a mile away from school, and Diana and I usually walked to and fro together. There was a pair of identical twins in the year above me, who used to fight each other in the playground, and I can remember telling my younger sister that this was something we would never do. If we had a disagreement, it would be between ourselves, I said, and only fishwives and street-girls ever used their fists. We were almost always very good friends, as we were with John, though he was four years my senior. He had a really wicked sense of humour, and would often have us in stitches. In my Lower Fifth year, Diana and I were confirmed by the Bishop of Whitby in Saltburn Parish Church, and Ping convinced my father (with his Methodist upbringing) that it was high time he also was confirmed. He became a churchwarden, and often took the collection plate up to the altar. Many times in church, John would get the giggles, and once he started it was so catching we could not stop. I also remember him saying once in an aside to my father, "Fingers out of the plate, Finkelbaum …" This saying, and others similar, became part of Werry folklore.

The old organist of the parish church, Mr W.S. Russell, used to let me play around on the organ, though I never had lessons then. I can just remember it was a large Victorian instrument, and I would sit at the console and try to get the feel of the entire keyboard for my feet. I did have some flute lessons with a teacher in Stockton, as we found we had an old wooden flute. I was never very good, though I could sight-read well, but played more when we moved South.

During our North Riding years our holidays had been cheap and fun. We all went Youth Hostelling in the Yorkshire Dales and the Lake District, and we had some wonderful times together with our dog. Many of the hostels were extremely primitive, but that added to the excitement. I remember Crossthwaite, high up on the fells. The YHA building was an old converted chicken farm. There was no electric light in the dormitory, and only cold running water, so when I fell off the top bunk in the night, and with difficulty found a piece of lint for the cut on my forehead, it was not until daylight that I realised the bandage was on the wrong way round and was stuck to my face ... We all remember torrential rain at Borrowdale, and getting wet through. We also visited Ambleside and Hawkshead, usually walking about five miles a day. The limestone caves at Ingleborough and Malham were simply wonderful, and we had such opportunities for talking to each other and telling stories.

We made one holiday visit to Devon, soon after we'd moved to Saltburn, to visit my Granny and Pater (my father's stepfather) in their house in Plymouth. We also paid a touching visit to the old folks' home in Okehampton, where Ping's Aunty Lizzie had been living since her brother Arthur (Ping's father) had died, of prostate cancer, in January 1943. By this time Aunty Lizzie was quite blind, and I remember her talking to John but looking in quite the wrong direction. This really upset me, and later when we took her for a drive and she thought she could see light and shade, I realised she couldn't see anything at all.

"Uncle" William Hoskins came to stay with us several times in Saltburn (and, great wine buff that he was, introduced us to wine for the very first time). We also had visits from some lady-friends of Ping's from Edmonton (Nancy Thompson and Ethel Hopkins), and we began to think about the possibility of moving to the South.

In Festival of Britain year (1951) we made our first trip to London, spending a whole day at the Festival site on the South

Bank. There were countless exhibitions and demonstrations taking place on the huge site, and hundreds and hundreds of people milling about. We children were allowed to go anywhere we wanted – and we agreed to meet hours later at a certain point. I found myself drawn towards the newly built Royal Festival Hall, and spent the entire afternoon listening to a Bach recital by the pianist Maurice Cole.

The following week, after we had done a lot of sightseeing in the city, we caught a night ferry (an eight-hour crossing then) from Dover to Calais, and then took a train to Paris, where we were introduced to the wonders of French culture for the very first time. (I was fifteen, Diana was thirteen-and-a-half, John was nineteen, and he was able to join us in Paris for a few days). Of course, we climbed the Eiffel Tower, visited Notre Dame and learned a little about French history, and found some lovely cafés in the back streets where we had our first taste of French food. We were happy to let Ping, being bilingual, do all the talking … We travelled by SNCF as far south as Marseille that year, stopping at interesting towns like Avignon, Arles and Nimes, staying in extraordinary little hotels, and experiencing for the first time the "minuterie", which complicated night visits to the WC along a dark corridor.

On the eve of my fifteenth birthday, I wrote a letter to myself, to be opened on the eve of my twenty-fifth birthday. In it, I wrote of my worries about the future: this was the time of the Korean War, and every day the Redcar Evening Gazette was full of the horrors of the war. I was also scared that my brother John, who was just nineteen, would buy a motorbike. (He eventually bought a three-wheeler Bond minicar, and drove around to our great concern, ending up in a road accident on the A1 near Grantham. That put paid to the car.) I thought I would like to study in Leipzig – no idea why, but probably because I knew it was where Bach had spent most of his life. And I wrote of my undying love for the young curate, a pale Irishman named Charles Connor, one of the few in Saltburn who spoke the Queen's English.

In the event, I completely forgot about this letter at the appropriate time, and laughed when I did find it again.

Back again in Yorkshire, my father started to apply for posts in London, and in August 1952, just after my GCE results arrived, we moved house again. My father took up the Headship at Kingsley School, Glebe Place, Chelsea. This again was a co-ed secondary modern school, but the educational world was changing rapidly, and it was not long before he aspired to a Headship of one of the new comprehensive schools, which were beginning to replace the old system of secondary modern, technical (central) schools, and grammar schools. His time in Chelsea was very productive. He founded the Chelsea Schools' Music Festival, and with his rather grand governing body (including Dame Regina Evans, his Chairman of the Governors, the Hon. Mrs Gascoigne and Mrs Moberly-Bell) he hosted some very successful events. Later on, I remember Speech Days in Chelsea Town Hall, sitting on the platform with Diana in our best dresses.

During that late summer of 1952, Diana and I stayed with the Stansfields in their lovely big house – Scotts' Hill House, Ware. They had an orchard full of apple trees; and it was a revelation to us to be living in such a spacious house with an imposing drive and big wrought-iron gates. (But there was one event we would rather forget: accidentally, a bright-red lipstick was ground into a white bedroom carpet upstairs, and the atmosphere cooled, despite our profuse apologies.)

Malham, Yorks.,
Easter 1949

Walking in the Dales, 1949

Upleatham Church, Cleveland,
1950. All of us with Granny

St Hilda's House, Saltburn H.S., 1950

John, Apprentice Officer, 1951

Newcastle Festival, 1951

Nimes Amphitheatre, 1951

Sunday afternoon on Wandsworth
Common with cousins Geoff Goff and
Christine Goff, 1952

74 St Ann's Hill, SW18, 1952

All of us in Wandsworth, 1953

Polyphotos, Elizabeth, 1954

Steeple Barton (chez Hoskins) 1953

Diana, John and Elizabeth, 1954

John's wedding to Pamela Hall, Guisborough, 1954

Orchestral Group, Datchelor, 1954

Datchelor Music Sixth, 1954

Roy and Iris, Aiguebelle, 1954

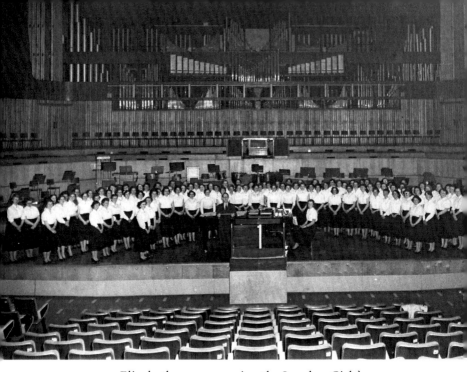

Elizabeth accompanying the London Girls'
Schools' Choir, RFH 1955

Harold Darke's Organ Scholars
(Corpus, Girton, Clare, St John's,
Selwyn, Jesus), 1955

Diana, 1955, 1st Prize in the
Spelling Bee – her prowess with Sir
Walter Scott won the day; Elizabeth
beaten into 2nd place over "cuirass"

Breakfast at Grantchester,
Nigel Graham Maw, 1956

Girton Ball, 1957,
Christopher Keyte, Nigel,
Elizabeth, Vanessa Parker

CUWBC, 1957

Picnic at Grantchester, 1957

Long Vac, 1957

Cricket: Girton XI v. King's Choir, May 1958. Back row left, Martin Briggs, Christopher Keyte. Far right, Bob Tear. Front row 4th left, Vanessa Parker. Centre, Robin Boyle next to Elizabeth.

London

Of course, that autumn we had to change schools yet again, and this time we found a really good old-established girls' voluntary-aided grammar school, governed by the Clothworkers' Company – the Mary Datchelor Girls' School in Camberwell Grove, SE5. The school was opened in 1877, established through a bequest from Mistress Mary Datchelor who died in 1725. The moment we arrived in London, the world seemed to open up before us. I was ready for a change, and determined to do well in the sixth form of a new, smart school with a reputation. Since 1877 the school had had only two headmistresses, the second of whom (Dame Dorothy Brock) did great things for girls' education, and in particular for Datchelor. (I later learned that Dame Dorothy was a Girtonian, and a friend of Rupert Brooke when they were fellow undergraduates.) When Diana and I joined the school in September 1952, Dame Dorothy had only just retired, and still appeared on important occasions. She was succeeded by Miss Rachel Pearse, a distinguished Quaker lady who had tremendous presence; she could hold the attention of the whole school while she spoke from the distant platform in front of the organ, in a quiet voice but one which carried to the very back of the balcony. She was like a ship in full sail walking slowly through the Hall at the beginning of daily Prayers, and was held in great regard by the 750 or so girls in the school.

We found a house in Wandsworth (74 St Ann's Hill, SW18), midway between my father's school in Chelsea and our own in Camberwell. And so we all moved in to this Victorian end-of-terrace corner house, together with a Bechstein grand, and two puppies acquired in Saltburn – Whisky (black and white, of course) and Brumas (mostly brown, but so named after a little bear at the London Zoo). Although it was a comfortable enough house, and wherever we lived our home was cosy, this house had no running hot water, and in the bathroom there was an Ascot gas-fired geyser which supplied bathwater. There was no central heating, but in those days not many houses did have it. We had an open fireplace, burning coal, which had to be delivered in sacks to the tiny backyard where there was an outside loo (rarely used, as there was another upstairs). The music-room had two outside walls, which meant that the room got very cold, and I remember practising late in the evening with just a single bar electric fire to take the chill off the room.

Across the road (St Ann's Hill) there was a primary school where the children would repeat their times tables parrot-fashion; with the windows open, this could be heard all down the street (Swaffield Road, known to the locals as "Bomb Alley" for obvious reasons). Every morning, Diana and I would leave the house at ten-to-eight, walk up to Earlsfield Road for the 77 bus, and then either change to the 35 to Brixton, then the 45 to Camberwell Green, or stay on the 77 to Wandsworth Road station and catch a train to Denmark Hill, and walk down the hill, along Grove Lane, to school. There were still trams in Wandsworth Road at that time.

I had a wonderful three years at Datchelor and have some very happy memories of excellent teaching there. My interest in English was fostered by the outstanding Head of the English

Department (Miss Nora Swithenbank) and there were some great characters among the staff, many of whom had lost fiancés in the First World War and had devoted their whole teaching lives to the same school. As well as "Swith", among these dedicated ladies were also Miss Gibson (Music), Miss Leask (French), Miss Fairlie (Maths), Miss Kett (Chemistry) and Miss Craze (Latin). But for me the importance of the school was the fact that the Music Sixth Form had been established by Miss Margaret Donington many years before I arrived on the scene, and this was my reason for going to the school.

At the end of the Lower Sixth year, a few of us had the chance to stand along the processional route for the Queen's Coronation, and I was fortunate to win a place. It meant getting to school that morning (June 2nd, 1953) at 5a.m., armed with sandwiches and a drink (and a mackintosh). We stood at the junction of Northumberland Avenue and the Embankment, and it was all very exciting. Very few people had television in those days (only one girl in my form did – Annella Kuyjpens, whose father was a French polisher). Later that month, the Queen and Prince Philip toured Camberwell in an open car, and the whole school lined Denmark Hill in our summer dresses (yellow, pink, blue, green or mauve, with white collars) to cheer them as they passed by. During my Lower Sixth year, I changed my mind about going to the Academy, having failed to win an Open Scholarship. I decided to opt for university entrance, and do English and French in addition to music.

I began to have piano lessons with Harold Craxton, at his Hampstead studio (14 Kidderpore Avenue) on Saturday mornings. This was a huge room at the back of the Craxton's big old Victorian house where there were two grand pianos and a gallery upstairs at one end. The studio and the hall were decorated with large murals by their son, John Craxton, who lived on a Greek island. Harold Craxton was the most admired professor at the Academy, and I was very fortunate to have him as my teacher for seven years, during which time I kept a notebook of my lessons, and would write each one up in it as I went home (on the 28 bus back to Wandsworth, while I was at school). His fees were three guineas a lesson (which was expensive then).

At school that term we had a Coronation Concert, and I played for a gifted violinist (Elizabeth Harding, later Lloyd-Davies, who became a very good friend). She played Handel's D major sonata on this occasion, and I can remember going to Max Rostal's house for a scary lesson before the concert. She subsequently went to the Guildhall to continue studying with him.

I began to play the organ, and also took my first piano diploma (LRAM Performer) that Spring. For this I played a Bach Prelude and Fugue in D, Bk II ("The Little Trumpeter"), Beethoven's "Moonlight" Sonata, Op. 27, and a Chopin Nocturne in E flat, Op. 55, no. 2. When I went in to play to the Board of three examiners, they said, "We'll start with the last movement of the Beethoven" (presto agitato): a baptism of fire … But Harold Craxton phoned that evening to tell me I'd passed with Honours.

Ping began to teach French again, at Clapham County Girls' School, and at last we were able to buy an old car, a 1938 Rover we nicknamed Peg (short for Pegasus, of course). In the summer holidays, we now began to go off on long holidays abroad, and we drove all over Europe.

We always left England on holiday with a car boot full of books to read. There was no shortage of reading material in our house, and in between the many visits to cathedrals, museums and art galleries, I read long wordy books such as "Hypatia" (Kingsley), "Henry Esmond" (Thackeray), and "The Cloister and the Hearth" (Kingsley).

We remember so many adventures from these trips – the opera "Aida" at Verona, sitting in the amphitheatre holding our lighted candles; di Stefano apologising in the first interval for missing his top B flat; the opera finishing so late (1a.m.?) that we decided to drive through the night to Venice without sleep. One year my father drove up over the Simplon Pass, with our old car boiling every so often. It was hilarious, but probably quite a worry for the driver. We also visited Spain one summer (probably my Upper Sixth year), and I was sending home to Gibby (our diminutive Head of the Music Department) my Licentiate Theory Papers for her to mark during the vacation. Another time we visited Mallorca, and stayed in a villa at Portocristo owned by an eccentric Danish painter, Christina. This was the beginning of a lifelong love of the island: as well as the limestone caves nearby, we visited Chopin's hideaway at Valldemossa for the first time.

Every summer holiday ended with a channel crossing by ferry, and the drive home to find exam results waiting on the mat.

My brother was happy in the Merchant Navy, only coming back from Africa for a few weeks every three months. He attended the King Edward VII Nautical School in the Mile End Road while he was home. We had some good times when he was around at weekends, and my best friend from school, Vivian Trower, came over. We would take the dogs up to Wandsworth Common, and all have a lot of laughs and fun together. Our weekends were usually fully occupied with homework, piano practice and a lesson in Hampstead on Saturday morning.

Then often we went to a matinée at the Old Vic. We must have seen every Shakespeare play, from the most well-known to the unusual ones, like "Timon of Athens" and "Coriolanus". The actors of the day included Paul Schofield, Donald Wolfit, Claire Bloom, Peggy Ashcroft and Virginia McKenna, to mention only a few. Tickets cost six shillings.

On Sundays we usually went to Sung Eucharist at St Anne's, the huge pepper-pot church at the High Street end of our road, where the vicar was the Rev. Charles Shells, who became a good friend. Then after Sunday lunch we would exercise the animals, either locally or on Wimbledon Common.

Sadly, one of the puppies (Whisky) was killed by a car, but Brumas lived for many more years, and was particularly loved by Viv and her sister Jean. John's girlfriend (Pamela Hall, a Saltburn High School girl a year above me) lived in Redcar, and they married in September 1954. We all went up to Guisborough for the wedding, and I remember Uncle Bill Goff came over from Sheffield too.

During this term, Diana and I were invited to a Sixth Form Dance at Emmanuel School by a local boy, Brian Seward, whom we knew from St Anne's Church. Brian was a year ahead of me, and heading for Imperial College for Maths, I think. We duly went along with him to this event on a cold winter evening, and stood or sat around in the vast school hall, looking like wallflowers and feeling ill-at-ease. Despite the ballroom dancing lessons we had had at the little studio on East Hill (learning foxtrot, quick step, waltz and so on – even tango), at this stage we felt little inclination or aptitude for this kind of activity. Brian offered to take us to see the Sixth Form Common Room (a luxury we did not have at Datchelor) and there we found a large display of interesting books: politics and history, I remember. Among these was a graphically illustrated book about the concentration camps of World War II, which until then we knew nothing about. This was less than ten years after the end of the war, and the horrific photographs of Belsen and Auschwitz survivors were just becoming more widely known. Of course, we discussed this at home immediately after that evening. Shortly after this, Anne Frank's father came to Datchelor to talk to a group of us in the Sixth Form. He was the sole survivor of the family. We all read "Anne Frank's Diary", and were deeply affected, especially as she was so near us in age.

Diana decided to do Medicine (to the amazement of all at school, as she had been top of all the Arts subjects at "O" level.) In those days the requirements for medical school were four "A" levels – Physics, Chemistry, Botany and Zoology, so she had her work cut out before going to Westminster Medical School (via King's in the Strand for 1ˢᵗ MB) the year after I left school.

By this time, my father had been appointed to the Headship of Tollington Park, a new co-ed Comprehensive in Islington, the amalgamation of three existing schools. He was given a year to prepare the timetable and staffing arrangements. This was to be a most successful move for him, eventually resulting in a CBE "for Services to Education", following a School Inspection.

But before all this excitement, we had years of exams as we progressed through Datchelor to the third year Sixth.

One of our unforgettable teachers was Annette Leask, who taught me French to "A" level. We studied Racine ("Andromaque"), Corneille ("Le Cid"), Molière ("L'Avare"), Balzac ("Eugenie

Grandet"), Victor Hugo ("Ruy Blas") and the short stories of Maupassant. Miss Leask's lessons were entertaining, to say the least, and she sometimes regaled us with tales of her Oxford tutor, who apparently had had a vision (officially verified by the Psychical Society!) of Marie Antoinette in the gardens of Versailles. This in all seriousness, and nobody dared smile …

In English, too, our literature lessons with Miss Swithenbank encouraged us all to read widely, not just Milton, Browning and "Antony and Cleopatra", the set works.

One of my contemporaries at school, Isolde Grove, was, very conveniently, the daughter of a viola player in the Royal Opera House Orchestra at Covent Garden. Thus we were able to have tickets for first performances of "Troilus and Cressida" (Walton), "The Turn of the Screw" and "Gloriana" (Britten), as well as rehearsal tickets for "The Trojans" (Berlioz), and long, long evenings of the complete "Ring" cycle. Perhaps it was those gallery slips benches that put me off Wagner for ever. I do remember catching a very late night bus all the way to Garratt Lane, and then walking up Swaffield Road to St Ann's Hill. It was dark and quiet in those empty streets, but we never felt it was dangerous in those days to travel alone.

In my Upper Sixth year I played the organ more often for school events, such as Prize Day or Prayers services, and sometimes at school concerts. On a Saturday afternoon in the summer term, my examiner for Grade 8 Organ was the composer and organist Harold Darke, and after my exam he asked me if I would like to turn for him at his next recital at St Michael's, Cornhill. I still have the programme: it was his 1035th Monday lunchtime recital at the City church where he was the Director of Music.

Soon after this, he became my organ teacher and I took ARCO around then, and joined his choir (The St Michael's Singers) which gave regular concerts in the City.

Life was busy and fun, and I decided to go for Oxbridge entrance. St Hugh's offered me a place for music at Oxford, which I accepted, but later turned down in favour of Girton. I took ARCM (Teacher's Diploma) that year – in those days it was usual to take these diplomas while still at school. Despite little real teaching practice, apart from helping Diana get a Merit in her Grade 7 Piano, and coaching my great friend Viv for her RCM entrance, I did pass, but certainly made up for lack of teaching experience later on.

Every Friday after school, I would go to the Lyons Corner House at Camberwell Green, and have baked beans on toast and a cup of tea. Then I would catch the 12 bus up to County Hall, where Dr Leslie Russell (Chief HMI for London) conducted a Girls' Choir, the London Schools' Girls' Choir, with singers from schools all over the city. I was the Choir's accompanist, and we did some good concerts and broadcasts, and learned some interesting pieces by Schubert, Brahms, Kodaly, Stanford, Vaughan Williams and others.

Dr Russell also conducted the London Schools' Symphony Orchestra, in which I played a rather poor 6th Flute, sitting in front of Alan Hacker (clarinet) who became a good friend. We had holiday courses, and I remember particularly one held at Archbishop Tenison's Grammar School, where we played Dvorak's 4th Symphony in G major, Op. 88, the Hary Janos Suite of Kodaly, and Hamisa Dor played the Elgar 'cello concerto. In one concert, Eileen Broster played Beethoven's 3rd piano concerto. Howard Snell was principal trumpet in the LSSO at that time, and he was also a very good pianist, sightreading a piano reduction of Stravinsky's "Rite of Spring" with tremendous aplomb.

I began to realise what a career in music might entail with these bright sparks all around. I savoured the opportunities that were given at Datchelor, and tried to make the most of my remaining time at school. I often used to think about my Granny's favourite quotation, which she wrote in my autograph book – Polonius's words to the young Hamlet:

> "Those friends thou hast, and their adoption tried,
> Grapple them to thy soul with hoops of steel."

Many years later I wrote some reminiscences for the Datchelor Old Girls' Newsletter:

"Memories of the Music Sixth

I arrived at Datchelor in September 1952, from the far-distant North Riding of Yorkshire. My memories of the little seaside town midway between Whitby and Middlesbrough are dominated by recollections of the biting winds as we played hockey on the icy beach. The years we spent there at the local girls' high school mercifully faded rapidly when we knew we were moving to London. At the time I was heading for the Royal Academy of Music, and the then HMI for Music recommended Datchelor as the best London school for sixth form music. What a culture shock. The moment my sister Diana and I climbed the steps to meet Miss Pearse – grand staircase with embossed shields, huge great hall with an ORGAN – and when I saw my timetable …!

In those days the Music Sixth Forms prepared girls to go on to one of the Conservatories (Royal Academy, Royal College or Guildhall) or to a Training College specialising in the teaching of music, or to a university to do a Music Degree. It was really the forerunner of the later specialist music departments of Wells, the Purcell or the Menuhin schools and had been set up by Margaret Donington, who went on to found the GRSM course at the Royal Academy. Aspiring musicians came to Datchelor from as far away as Harrow (Villia Harper, violin), Mill Hill (Maureen Webb, piano), Orpington (Eileen Burrell, singing), Finchley (Chrystalla Yiallouri, violin), Beckenham (Fiona Ross, singing), Birmingham (Elizabeth Harding, violin) and Hampstead (Diana Cummings, violin). These are only a few of the many I remember who became professional musicians.

Our five-day week timetable consisted of seven lessons each day, all related to aspects of musical training. There was **Harmony**, which was largely the study of Bach chorales and **Counterpoint** comprising five species, increasingly difficult when you got beyond two-part writing. There was also the **History and Literature of Music**. Here we covered Gregorian chant through mediaeval and renaissance music and the Tudor period, right up to major 20th century figures such as Bartok, Elgar, Sibelius and Britten. Jane Short also took us for **Aural Training** and boring old **Rudiments**, covering everything from intervals and part writing to Italian and German expressions and complicated ornaments.

Where our course at Datchelor differed, however, was in the range of music we encountered through our **Ensemble** classes, when we sight-read at two pianos, Haydn, Mozart, Beethoven and even Brahms Symphonies. Invaluable as a help to those whose reading wasn't great, this introduced us to a wide repertoire at a time when we had actually heard very little. Then there was **Improvisation**, where I can remember playing in the style of, say, Mozart, with Miss Gibson on the other piano leading one into more and more adventurous keys. The gradual improvement in our improvisation was tremendously helpful when it came to our "assisting" in the Music and Movement lessons of the first formers in the Dalcroze Technique training in the Bath Hall. One or other of us had to provide suitable music for "Storms"/"Raindrops"/"Waves"/"Fairies" and so on, whatever was demanded by the mistress in charge (was it Miss Haynes?) This was only a little less scary than the ordeal of training one's own special First Form to compete in the annual choral competition held in the School hall. Teaching a two-part song (I remember "Daffodils" by Eric Thiman) was hard enough for a 16- to 17-year-old: keeping order in a class of wriggly 11-year-olds probably harder. I do seem to remember, though, that my form was Sheila Rogers' class, and they were usually well behaved!

Apart from Singing in the Hall, most of our lessons took place in Music Room A. Here we also had what we called "Choral" – about twelve of us, across Lower, Upper and Third Year Sixth – singing quite complex unaccompanied pieces, the sort of anthem needed for an important Service such as the Induction of the new Master of the Clothworkers' Company, always held in June at St Olave's Church in Hart Street, EC.

In the Upper Sixth we were given passes to attend the Royal Philharmonic Society rehearsals and concerts in the Royal Festival Hall, and we were able to watch Beecham at work with the RPO. Another unforgettable experience was the opportunity to sing the chorales each Easter in the *St Matthew Passion*, and I can remember singing with Reginald Jacques in the Royal Albert Hall and with Paul Steinitz (in German) at St

Bartholomew the Great, Smithfield. Of course, all Datchelor girls remember, probably above every other musical experience at school, our own performances of *Messiah*, which were so carefully prepared, with the Senior Choir doing the hardest bits and a few tenors and basses joining us at the last rehearsal. How lucky we were to be introduced to so much. There was always a big anthem on Prize Day – my old programmes remind me of "Sound the Trumpet" (Purcell) and "Shine out, great Sun" (Handel); a huge task for tiny Miss Gibson and later Mary Rose Seldon to control and inspire 700 girls and a large orchestra led by the redoubtable Amy Neame.

I am constantly reminded how lucky we all were to have such musical experiences in our formative years. As it turned out, I did a couple more A-levels at Miss Pearse's suggestion, and opted for Cambridge where I became an organ scholar. I am greatly indebted to Miss Swithenbank for introducing me in particular to the wonders of Milton and Browning (did she sow the seed of my later forming a Reading Group, I wonder?) and also to Miss Leask with her inimitable stories of the ghosts of Versailles (to say nothing of Racine, Corneille, Victor Hugo and Maupassant).

I cannot, however, leave my reminiscences of music at Datchelor without mentioning the opening of the Royal Festival Hall organ in the presence of HM the Queen Mother. As a budding organist I got the chance to present the bouquet on this occasion, thanks to someone with influence at County Hall having come to a Datchelor concert shortly before this event. Later, with the Choir, which accompanied the London Schools' Symphony Orchestra, I did play the new organ – Vaughan Williams' "Old Hundredth" – with the venerable old man sitting listening in one of the boxes.

All of us are sad that the old School is no more, and the memories we have crowd in upon us as we get older, especially when we hear some evocative hymn or words that remind us of Christmas Lunch in the Dining Hall (remember the Boar's Head Carol?) – or singing "Honour Wisdom" to Miss Donington's unforgettable tune, or remembering the way we whispered the Lord's Prayer each morning.

Long may the spirit of Datchelor music echo in St Olave's when we next meet for Carols."

In June every year, the Senior Choir would prepare an Anthem to sing at a special service at the Church of St Olave Hart Street, in the City, for the Induction of the new Master of the Clothworkers' Company.

We would travel by bus through the area around St Paul's, which had not yet then been completely rebuilt. There was still a lot of war-damage visible from the top of the bus. Many churches were still unrepaired, and there were piles of rubble still visible in the City churchyards. But St Olave's was one of the first churches to be restored, and it always seemed to be sunny when we were there. The walls were newly white, there were some new stained glass windows, and a new organ had been installed. The clothworkers, governors of our school, were always very friendly to us, and gave us many named prizes on Prize Day. I also had a leaving Exhibition from them for £40.

We were very receptive during these formative years, and strongly influenced by words of wisdom from our elders.

Our School song, "Wisdom", was composed in 1939 by Mary Donington, with words from the Wisdom of Solomon:

"O God of the fathers give me wisdom, give me wisdom
"Passing into holy souls she maketh men the friends of God.
"Honour wisdom, Honour wisdom.
"For there is in her a spirit of understanding, loving what is
good, unhindered, steadfast, sure.

"Honour wisdom, Honour wisdom.
"To know the beginning and end and middle of times.
"The circuits of years, and the placing of stars,
"The natures of living creatures, the ragings of wild beasts.
"The violence of winds and the thoughts of men –

"Honour wisdom. Honour wisdom.
"Wisdom is more mobile than any motion,
"An unspotted mirror of the working of God.

"Oh God of the fathers, give me wisdom, give me wisdom,
give me wisdom."

Selected from the Book of Wisdom

Miss Pearse's thoughtful talks to us in the third year Sixth, when we would sit in a circle in her room, made us realise and accept that from those to whom much was given, much was expected. The traditions of service to others had been fostered by the School's Dorcas Society, which made garments for the poor. Everyone in the School took part each year. Knitting or sewing something, even if it was only some bedsocks for an old lady in Love Walk, a home supported by the School.

As my last year at School was finishing, I was very aware that a chapter was about to end. Whatever lay ahead for me in Cambridge, I knew I'd had a good start, even if I were not yet quite that Fine Lady.

Cambridge

Cambridge – my spiritual home. What comes into my head first?

The bend in the river at Grantchester perhaps, the meadows bursting with buttercups in May, the orchard crowded with apple trees; punting back to King's in time for Evensong on Sunday afternoon; battling up Castle Hill in the rain; supervision with Hugh McLean on Purcell, and with crusty old Hubert Middleton on W.P. Kerr and Suzanne Langer; rehearsing the Chapel Choir in Woodlands Court; Girton Lake in the snow; those long, long corridors with no central heating, and the pitiful little electric fire I had in my first year; my 21st party in the Stanley Library; Honeysuckle Walk in June; singing madrigals in the punts moored by King's Bridge in May Week as the light gradually faded, crowds lining the Backs, as we sang Finzi's "My Spirit Sang All Day", and always Gibbons' "The Silver Swan" before the end. Yes, of course, all these things drift through my mind.

But then, I remember that winter when I had accepted a place at St Hugh's, and had gone up to Oxford to sit the Qualifying Exam in Music, which all girls were required to pass before taking up residence. It was a very cold spring that year, and this was the beginning of March. I spent a night with my historian "Uncle" William Hoskins (then a Fellow of All Souls) who lived in a lovely old vicarage at Steeple Barton. Next day, after my exam in the Music Faculty (subfusc. and all), I took a train to Bedford, en route for an interview in Cambridge, only to find when I got to Bedford that there were no further trains to Cambridge till the next day. Well, this was an emergency, I thought, and the £30 my father had given me must be put to good use. So I hailed a taxi, and arrived in the late evening at Girton College, a very imposing building on the Huntington Road, with huge gardens and a long drive up to the Tower and the Porter's Lodge.

In those days, it was possible to sit the Oxford exams in November, and also to take the Cambridge papers in February, even having accepted a place at Oxford. This is what I did, and so I arrived at Girton College in the dark, suitably impressed and rather intimidated. I had my interview with the Director of Studies in Music the following morning, tried the Chapel organ, and then caught the bus into town. I knew nothing about Cambridge. At the time there were no Open Days – this was my first visit. We were still using Ration Books, and ten years after WW2 this was austerity Britain.

Getting off the bus at St John's, I wandered down Trinity Street, overawed by all I saw on either side. Then suddenly I looked up and the pinnacles of King's Chapel were visible ahead. I did not know what this building was, but decided to go and investigate. It was cold and windy, and the moment I went inside was an absolute revelation. When I go into the Chapel now, I am still filled with a tremendous sense of wonder. In those far-off days, the chapel ceiling was black from years of candlewax, yet even then the windows sparkled and their bright colours were reflected on the stonework. For me this was the deciding moment. I accepted my place at Girton and never looked back.

The Music Faculty was, and still is, quite small, and with a couple of students a year in most of approximately twenty-two Colleges, we soon knew everyone. One of the girls in Diana's form at school was Elisabeth Keyte, a harpist, and her brother Christopher, an Alleyn's boy, was a Bass choral scholar at King's. He became a firm friend and through him I got to know all the choir, joined the Madrigal Society, conducted by Boris Ord, and later by Raymond Leppard. We rehearsed in the Chetwynd Room in King's. The choral scholars had rooms in Gibbs Building, at 13 King's Parade, and on the staircases down by the river.

I was swept into all things musical, and from my first term there was scarcely an empty moment. We didn't have many lectures to attend, and academic life for me centred around weekly supervisions with my Director of Studies (Jill Vlasto), and a couple of others for different subjects, such as composition (with Prof. Patrick Hadley at Caius) and counterpoint (with George Guest at St John's). The best lecturers were Philip Radcliffe (King's) who invariably illustrated his lectures on nineteenth century literature at the piano entirely from memory, and also John Stevens (Magdalene) who enthused over mediaeval English ballads at 9 a.m. on a Monday morning. That these English Faculty lectures were attended by so many musicians was testament to his brilliance as a lecturer. Others were not as popular – Peter Tranchell (King's), for instance, was boring in the extreme, talking about Poulenc operas. For the most part, we were left to get on by ourselves, use the libraries and play lots of records. In Part I of the Tripos we studied all the seven Symphonies of Sibelius, and I remember lovely long afternoons at 13 King's Parade just listening to them.

As an Organ Scholar, I played for Chapel every morning at ten to eight (wearing my slipsocks in the cold weather), and practised when I had time for the FRCO exam which I would take at the Royal College of Organists in Kensington. In my first year, my organ teacher, Harold Darke, came up to play at Clare one evening. Six of us (his organ scholar pupils) took him out to dinner afterwards, and the next morning at 7.30 a.m. we had a photo taken outside King's chapel (where he had been director of music during the war). The following year David Willcocks arrived from Worcester to take over from the ailing Boris Ord as Director of Music at King's, and I was able to have some lessons with him on the King's organ before taking my FRCO. I believe for that exam I played, as well as some Bach, something by Saint-Saëns, and a Hindemith Sonata. Anyway, I did well enough to pass, and that was my final organ exam ever. In those days, we had a modest 2-manual Harrison tracker-action instrument in Girton chapel, so it was a huge thrill to be invited later on to play a Saturday evening post-Evensong Recital in King's during my last May Week.

As music students, we spent a lot of time singing in various small groups, usually conducted by very keen organ scholars who needed sopranos that could sightread, as rehearsal time was always very limited. But occasionally there would be a big performance by an ambitious conductor like Michael Brimer (Clare) who once conducted us (the Clare Canaries) in the St Matthew Passion in Great St Mary's.

In my very first term I joined a double quartet in Pembroke, conducted by Nigel Graham-Maw, a law student in his second year, who had already done Part I Modern Languages. This group was called the Valence Mary Singers, and I happily joined them in the concerts and festivals they took part in. Alan Mayall was one of the tenors (later winning the prestigious Richard Tauber Singing Prize), and this was an established little choir, strongly supported by Meredith Dewey, the wonderful Dean of Pembroke, such a staunch friend later. Little did I imagine when I joined the Valence Mary Singers that I would marry the conductor about six years later.

The Singers had taken their name from Marie de Valence, Countess of Pembroke (the foundress of the College in 1347) and in whose memory we held an annual dinner in Meredith's rooms. He had a fine collection of books, music and old porcelain, and a lovely Bechstein grand. His rooms overlooked the Dean's garden, one of the gems of Pembroke. Meredith was a botanist as well as a cleric, and had a constant stream of past students visiting him with their families, as we did later on. He used to say that our generation (the Billy Graham years, up to 1960) was conventional. We attended Chapel, we accepted authority and so on, and that the next decade saw a complete overthrow of accepted standards. By the time of the "mixed staircases" revolution of the 70's, everything was different.

We had very few rules at Girton, apart from signing out if we were going to be in later than 10 p.m. (The deadline was midnight). Men had to be out of Girton by 10 p.m. (the College went co-ed in 1979). A few adventurous undergraduates would "climb in" through ground-floor windows (pre-arranged with a co-operative friend) if they hadn't got special permission to be out late. But we were a pretty law-abiding bunch, nobody had much money, and we were quite serious about work. The musicians always had so much to occupy them, with constant rehearsals for concerts in other colleges desperate for sopranos. (The ratio then was ten men to one woman). We also had our own practice to do – music students generally had a piano in their room – and of course I had to take choir practice for Sunday chapel services. This was before the days of choral scholarships at Girton (or the Instrumental Awards Scheme), so I had to canvass for choir members. Occasionally we sang short anthems (women's voices only of course) at Evensong on Sundays – we used the Anglican Chant Book for the Psalms – but we were certainly not very ambitious musically. In my second year I decided to study a Bach Prelude and Fugue each week, and it took me two years (six terms of eight weeks each) to get through the whole of the '48, Books I and II.

Later, we were expected to develop a Portfolio of compositions for Part II of the Tripos. This could include such works as a string trio, an organ chorale-prelude, a verse anthem perhaps, some songs with piano accompaniment or virtually anything you wanted to compose. I remember Stanley Glasser wrote five unaccompanied madrigals – and got a First. Years after I came down, Philip Radcliffe quoted to me the theme from something I had written (I think it was the verse anthem à la Purcell which I must have shown him ten years earlier). It was certainly no great composition; he just had this remarkable memory. He composed a delightful little organ piece ("Pastorale") for me on the occasion of my wedding in 1961. His responses were often sung in King's chapel, and I was so pleased, many years later, that he supervised Mary too when she was reading Music at Homerton College.

My Director of Studies (Jill Vlasto) was the librarian of the Rowe Music Library at King's. As an old Datchelor girl we had a lot in common, and she would often talk about her schoolfriend Daphne Bird, who directed the music course at Bretton Hall, Yorkshire. Jill lived in Adams Road, in one of those huge houses with large book-lined rooms looking on to an enormous garden where Alexandra and Dominic, then aged six and three, ran riot. Jill's husband Alexis was a Fellow of King's, later the librarian of

Selwyn, and his hobby was orchids, which sat on many of the window sills around the house. Jill was a very strong influence on me, and persuaded us to produce "Jephtha" (Carissimi) one year at Girton, and the next to play a Mozart Concerto (K491 in C minor) with an orchestra including players from several other colleges as we did not have enough orchestral players that year. In my last year we produced "Dido and Aeneas" (Purcell) in which my great friend Anne Keynes sang Dido. She and I were fellow sopranos in the Madrigal Society, and one summer we travelled to Amsterdam and Leiden to give a number of concerts conducted by Boris Ord – some in churches, one on a canal. Roger Norrington (Clare) was in the choir then, as were the Kingsmen Clifford Hughes and Christopher Keyte, and Nigel G.M.

These last three formed a quartet with me, which we called the Cambridge Consort, and we travelled around the south of England one summer giving concerts (of madrigals, solo songs, and piano solos) at schools where we had connections: Roedean, Westminster, Walthamstow Hall (Sevenoaks) and St James' West Malvern. I remember all of these with their varied atmospheres and colourful headmistresses. My best friend in College was Vanessa Parker (niece of the actor Cecil Parker), who arranged our visit to her old school St James', and this was a memorable visit. The headmistress was the grand Miss Anstruther, and the girls were mostly daughters of diplomats and socialites, not remotely interested in going to university. How Vanessa got to Girton on Physics and Greek "A" Level remained a mystery, but the authorities obviously recognised a brainy girl, who went on to do a Ph.D. in local history. Her book "The Making of King's Lynn" remains a classic in this field.

Most of my friends in College were historians and medics. The historians were under the guidance of Jean Lindsay, a formidable character, and Mrs Chibnall (the Chib). Mrs Lindsay's Historical Society Evenings were legendary: period costumes, food and all. Other famous dons were Muriel Bradbrook, a remarkable Elizabethan scholar who later became Mistress of the College, and Lady Jeffreys who, though she was a mathematician, took a great interest in musical matters in College. Another ageless character was Alison Duke, a classicist, who eventually left Girton a lot of money.

Acoustics was part of the Music Tripos, and we studied Sir James Jeans' book during our lectures in the Cavendish Laboratory, then in Free School Lane. Not having done Physics at school, this was difficult for me, and I was very happy to have some help from Colin Nicholls (Magdalene) who had already done Natural Sciences Part I and was having fun doing Music in his last year. An added attraction was that he had a little old car, falling to bits but just about roadworthy, and he would take me on jaunts to places like Ely Cathedral. There were so many places of interest nearby which were accessible by car, and I got to know some of the wool church villages of the Fens. Later, when I knew Nigel better, he would drive me and Vanessa on our brass-rubbing expeditions: East Anglia has many of the very best Flemish brasses, from Trumpington to Long Melford, and we would spend the whole day picnicking and exploring the villages.

In those days undergraduates under the age of twenty-two could not have a car, so this rule precluded most students from driving before their final year. Of course, until Suez (1956) all the men had done National Service, so were two years older than the girls anyway. Nigel had a little red open-topped MG (CLU 815) and later a black Morris Minor (TXU 317) On one famous occasion, he was driving his father's Bentley back up the A10 through Harston, and was stopped by the police for some minor infringement. He never tired later of relating how the policeman asked him, "Are you owner-driver of this car?"

Some undergraduates had a Vespa, and it was a help sometimes to be given a hand cycling up Castle Hill back to Girton. Along the Huntington Road were many large Victorian houses (some were College hostels). A number of Girton dons lived along this road, including Lady Jeffreys and later my tutor, Sheila Gillies who lived with the Molière scholar, Mme Odette de Mourgues. Old Mrs Rootham, widow of Cyril (of Rootham in E minor, still sung then at St John's) used to invite Girton musicians to tea on Sunday afternoons in her gloomy house, 105 Huntington Road. Here she would regale us with stories of the past and show us ancient photographs of bygone times. She must have been ninety if she was a day. But we lapped it all up, and were thrilled to be part of such a venerable crowd. We always wrote little thank-you letters after such visits, as instructed by Jean Lindsay's "Etiquette for Undergraduates" (prescribed reading).

The road out to Girton (three miles from town) only seemed a long way in bad weather. We musicians sometimes cycled that journey three times in a day, if we had a morning lecture (rare), an afternoon chamber music rehearsal (frequent), then after Evensong at King's, back for Hall at 7 p.m., then perhaps an evening concert, meeting or party (often). No wonder the College Song Book, always used after College Feasts, contains the popular ditty "three years at Girton, developing your personality and your calves" ...

New Hall and Fitzwilliam College buildings had not then appeared on the Huntington Road; the few New Hall girls were then living in Darwin's old house on Silver Street, and Fitz had an old Victorian redbrick house opposite the Fitzwilliam

Museum. Their glory days were yet to come. I had a school friend, Valerie Lewis, reading Modern Languages at New Hall (one of the first few students there), and a friend, also from school, who read English at Newnham. This was Eve Meckhonik, who later did a Ph.D. on Julian of Norwich; she married a writer, Brian Richards. For the most part my friends were Girtonians, or musicians from many of the other Colleges. One of my first new friends in College was the medic Marjorie Doddridge, whose father Jack had been at school in Plymouth with my father when they were boys of nine or ten. Marjorie became a very good friend, and I played for her wedding to Peter Corley (King's) in 1961. She asked me to play the March from a Suite by Cornelius as the final Voluntary. This caused great amusement to the many Cheltenham girls present, as this piece was invariably played at the end of term as they broke up for the holidays.

The standard of chamber music in Cambridge was high, and I was very fortunate, through the CU Music Club, to play with the best instrumentalists around. The violinist Colin Gough (Corpus) led the NYO before he came up to read Physics. We did numerous concerts together in Cambridge, at Oxford for their Music Society (in the Holywell Music Room), and later on in London at the Oxford and Cambridge Musical Club. But Colin, whose 'cellist brother Howard married the oboist Celia Nicklin, went on to become Professor of Astrophysics at Birmingham, and violin playing happily remained a hobby for him. Also from the NYO was my friend Jennifer Clapham (clarinettist), a medic for whom I played a lot. Other outstanding ex-NYO players were Guy Woolfenden (Christ's) and Tim Reynish (Caius), both horn players. The best keyboard players were Colin Tilney (harpsichord), Simon Preston (organ) and Philip Ledger – all Kingsmen.

One could easily have spent the whole of one's time as a student just playing chamber music, or accompanying singers, which was always a great joy for me. My two favourite singers in the King's Choir were Christopher Keyte and the tenor Robert Tear, and I remember so many memorable performances with them. One lunchtime Christopher and I performed Schumann's "Dichterliebe" in Queens' (the first of many solo recitals later), and I remember a Sunday evening recital in King's Hall with Bob and a string quartet led by Robin Morrish, doing "On Wenlock Edge" (Vaughan Williams). I can't remember now why I was playing for them because they were all Kingsmen. We were all good friends, and they had a little club called COI (Comedy Operas Inc.) at which we would sing through, very roughly, works like "The Pirates of Penzance" (G&S), usually in a room in King's, sitting around sightreading. One evening everyone creased up when we came to the words: "Yo ho, my trim-built wherry! ..." Well, we were only nineteen or twenty.

There was also another fine baritone at King's – Neil Howlett – who won the Ferrier Prize the year he went down, and of course became a well-known operatic singer. I also liked playing for the tenor Kenneth Bowen (St John's) who married my Girton friend Angela Evenden. Ken sang the part of Tom Rakewell in "The Rake's Progress" (Stravinsky) which we performed in the Arts Theatre in my third year, conducted by Leon Lovett (Magdalene) – also later married to another Girtonian, medic Eileen Hardy. That year, 1958, George Guest married Nancy, to everyone's delight. (George was still in charge of St John's Choir in 1990 when John G.M. was singing there as a Bass volunteer).

In my first Easter vacation, I took a job as a nanny looking after four grandchildren of a formidable old Girtonian, Margery

Spring-Rice, widow of a former Ambassador to Washington, Cecil Spring-Rice (author of "I vow to thee, my country"). Mrs Spring-Rice's daughter (also Cecil) was a Girtonian too, married to a Classics professor from Trinity. They were off on a Swan Hellenic cruise and had taken the eldest child with them, leaving the other four with grandmother (and me). We drove from their home in Hammersmith, squashed into a small shooting-brake, to the Spring-Rice home, Iken Hall, in Suffolk. This was a pretty remote old vicarage on the banks of the Iken River near Woodbridge. The children, aged twelve, nine, six and three, were lovely but quite unruly, and I was with them all day every day, climbing trees and stopping them from falling in the river. The house was cold and there was no running hot water.

It was quite an education for me – the house was filled with interesting books (complete Hardy in my bedroom) and lovely drawings, many of the children. I also remember a huge old HMV gramophone with a large speaker and turntable, on which we played old 78s. Benjamin Britten called in one day, and told me he had written "The Little Sweep" for the children of the house. I was actually quite glad when my three weeks came to an end, and I was able to go home (with my £9 salary).

That summer in the Long Vac, I went on a three-week cycling/camping trip with my historian friend Gay Theobald to Ireland, which neither of us had visited before. We had one contact near Cork, given us by Jill Vlasto, so we made for that house when we left the ferry, and put up our tent in the garden of this big mansion overlooking the sea. Thereafter we followed our map, and cycled with about 40lbs of equipment on each bike all around the south coast via Bantry Bay, then up into the Kerry mountains, through Killarney, Listowel, Limerick, Galway, and then turned West along the peninsula to the very remote villages where they spoke nothing but Gaelic.

We did have a few adventures: sleeping in a field once with a bull; buying trout from a fisherman, then not knowing quite how to cook it; wall-papering a room in a tiny cottage in the Black Valley in exchange for a bed for the night; having the odd puncture and getting very wet once or twice. But all in all it was an exhilarating trip, and arriving back at Paddington on the train, I cycled across town via Chelsea and called on my father at his school. When I knocked on his door and he said, "Come in," he did not even recognise me – I was so tanned, freckled, and probably very dirty.

Early in my time at Cambridge, I met Jim Ede, the Curator recently retired from the Tate. He moved to Kettle's Yard, two ancient cottages which he had converted into a beautiful space to display his collection of English watercolours by Ben and Winifred Nicholson, Alfred Wallis, and some lovely sculptures and drawings by Gaudier-Breszka. He was very generous with these paintings, and would lend them out to undergraduates, to be returned at the end of the term. He and Helen had a very good Bechstein grand, and I used to practise there most days. He started a series of cushion concerts, and there were lovely, informal gatherings where we all sat round on the stairs. I remember the pianist Denise Lassimone coming to play for us. Later we bought one of the Gaudier-Breszka drawings for £200. When Jim retired to Edinburgh he gave his entire collection and property to the University.

Jim Ede introduced me to the Camberwell artist Patrick Symons, who painted my portrait in 1961, and one of Nigel in 1967. He also did a pencil drawing of Jane, just before he was killed in Paris in 1993 while crossing the road.

Few of the musicians at Cambridge did much sport, as it was so time-consuming if you were serious about it. In my second year, I rowed for the CU Women's Boat (as Bow). This meant a lot of early mornings in the Lent Term (cold!) and a certain amount of dedication which for me was destined not to last very long. We rowed against Reading and London Universities (both of which races we won), but the Oxford race was called off as the Oxford Ladies had damaged their boat on the weir. So though I got my Colours shield, I had to forego a Half-Blue.

At the end of the season I decided enough was enough, but I kept a photograph from the Cambridge Evening News to show the family. Diana, too, rowed for Westminster Medical School that season, but we agreed it was not a sport for girls like us. In the summer term that year, however, I raised a Girton Cricket XI to play an informal match against the King's Choir, and this we greatly enjoyed as it was not taken too seriously.

Work in the third year got serious, with concentration on weekly supervisions for composition and literature (set works). Professor Patrick Hadley (who will forever be remembered for his exquisite carol "I sing of a maiden that is makeless") was my supervisor for part of my composition portfolio. Sadly, his WW1 leg injury left him more or less permanently in pain, and more often than not I would find a note on his door: "Prof. Hadley is indisposed today". Composition was never one of my strongest suits; I was much more interested in Palaeography and the History and Practice of Criticism, which, with Performance, were the other sections in the syllabus for the postgraduate course I wanted to do, known as Mus. B. Stanley Glasser (King's) who had already done at least one degree from Witwatersrand was the most gifted composer among us, and subsequently became Dean of Goldsmiths' College.

The summer terms always passed in a flash, and we would cycle everywhere in summer dresses, always wearing a gown after dark. If you were stopped by a "Bulldog" for leaving your gown behind, you would be summoned to appear before one of the Proctors at a specified time, in order to pay a fine. This happened to me only once, and I was requested to appear at Trinity one evening before Hall. I duly appeared, knocked on the door of a senior member of the College, had a lovely chat with him over a glass of sherry, and then was asked for 7/6d as I left!

There were very few weeks before the exams in May, and we did our revision in the gardens at Girton (always sunny, it seemed). We had 45 acres, so no shortage of space; a lake, a rose garden, an orchard, fields, a honeysuckle walk and plenty of grass to sit on. There were always the cool libraries of course, but I do remember some students sitting with their books on the Backs, with distractions all around.

Once the exams were over, and results posted on the Senate House boards, there would be a constant stream of students peering anxiously at the Tripos lists to find out how they had fared. Then, May Week! Concerts, parties, and the Balls. Not every College had a Ball every year, and usually there were groups of three or four Colleges to which your ticket allowed you access. If your loyalties were with a particular College, you soon felt your own special College Ball was the best, and you would gravitate back to it. How many flimsy shoes I ruined on the cobbles around Trinity, St John's and King's! As May Week is traditionally in the middle of June, you would think this would be a safe time for an out-of-doors event. But I remember several wet evenings among the nine or ten Balls I attended in my four years in Cambridge.

One year on the King's lawn there were several enormous braziers as it was such a damp evening. But we had Chris Barber's Skiffle Group that night, and a wonderful feast as always. And at Pembroke there was Tommy Kinsman's Band one year, and the Old Library was done up as a Charnel House. After the Survivors' photograph at 5 a.m., we punted up the river to have breakfast in the orchard at Grantchester. The pictures remind me that we were four in the party on that occasion: Diana and a partner from Westminster Medical School, and Nigel and myself. There was another Ball the following night (at King's) so by the time we went down the next day we were exhausted. But the Long Vac was over three months long, unless you were doing the Long Vac term (six weeks from early July), so there was time to recover.

Girton's Ball was always in March, and I recall there were others in the winter too, like the Cardinal's Ball. One winter I went to the Valentine's Ball at Caius with Robin Walton, whose hockey shirts I used to iron – why, I can't imagine: I suppose he didn't have an iron. He was a musician, but rather deaf, and joined the Colonial Service later on. I went to the Union Society once or twice with him, but found him boring. His father was Registrar of Manchester University.

These years never come again, and they are a time when life-long friendships are often made. This was certainly so for me. At the end of my third year, most of my contemporaries went down. The following term as a graduate, I sat on Little High in Hall, and made a new set of friends, some from other universities and countries. One was Isabel McBryde from Australia, doing a Diploma in Archaeology, subsequently becoming a Professor in Canberra. Another was Elinor Brightman, with a Double First from Edinburgh in English and Italian. She was doing a Ph.D. with C.S. Lewis on "The English Gentleman in Italian literature". She became a very good friend, and later married a St John's choral scholar, Christopher Bevan. They settled in Edinburgh and sadly rarely came South, but both of them worked for the British Council, and lived for years in such exotic places as Cairo and Thessalonika.

In his fourth year, Nigel was doing L.L.B. when I was doing Part II of the Music Tripos. Most of his close friends (Mike Nyren, Peter Corley and Martin Briggs, all Kingsmen) had gone down, and apart from his diligent study of the law (his filing system for revising cases was amazing), music played a very large part in his relaxation time. He played the clarinet in several College orchestras, including one Girton concert. He also rowed for Pembroke, though perhaps not in his fourth year. His father had coxed Pembroke's First Boat in 1920 when Pembroke was Head of the River in the May Bumps, so there was some incentive there. It was always great fun to stand on the towpath down by the Pike and Eel and cheer on the boats. Everyone dressed up in summer blazers and boaters with College colours.

Then, that summer, Nigel went down and began Articles to his father, for Solicitors' Finals. He started on a Gibson and Welldon course for help with some of the hard papers – Tort being very difficult, I believe. He was living at home, 21 Alleyn Park, Dulwich, and occasionally would drive up to Cambridge for the day and visit me. Once, he brought his mother and father up to Girton to have coffee on a Sunday morning in my room. I must have been nervous, because I can even remember what I was wearing. His father told me he had never been to Girton before, and I'm afraid he thought I was a blue-stocking. Perhaps I was. One evening we all had dinner at the University

Arms before spending an hour or so at the Pembroke Ball, but they left early for the long drive back to Dulwich.

My course for Mus.B. was the most interesting of my four years in Cambridge. I chose to do Performance as one of my two sections, and Palaeography and Criticism as the other. Ray Leppard was one of my supervisors, and a little group of us would go to his rooms in Trinity to discuss, for example, the idea of "Progress" as a concept. One day I remember we talked about, and listened to, Strauss's "Metamorphosen", and then had to write a critique of it.

Peter le Huray (St Catherine's) was the most impressive supervisor for the Palaeography paper: at the time he was writing a book on English Verse Anthems, which became a standard text for music students.

And then, there was Thurston Dart (Jesus). He was a pioneer in the editing and performance of early music, and a very popular lecturer. The Music School would be full to bursting with undergrads from all faculties, who wanted to know something about early instruments and the music written for them. Bob would play little pieces on a clavichord or a harpsichord, and often would play from manuscript copies he had just edited – John Bull, Tomkins, Purcell and Gibbons – on a little chamber organ, using "squeaky" stops (8', 4', and 2' stops).

He was a great character. Once he was playing the Goldberg Variations at a Selwyn College Sunday evening recital. Gerald Hendrie, the organ scholar, was turning the pages for him, and later told me that just as he was going onto the platform, Bob turned to him and said, "Utter up a prayer for me, old boy, I'm sightreading." Bob Dart also had a Consort of Viols with Jill and Alexis Vlasto and John Stevens. Sometimes their recitals were hilarious, with Alexis going wrong in about the fourth bar, and Bob saying majestically, "Shall we begin again?" But the early music movement was gaining in popularity, and soon Alfred Deller and Desmond Dupré came to perform at the Cambridge Union, and were very enthusiastically received. Thurston Dart (later Cambridge Professor) was a great help to me, advising me on my choice of recital pieces for my Performance exam; he got me interested in playing the Faculty harpsichord, firing my enthusiasm for continuo playing. His motto, which he often quoted to us, we applied to any unknown piece of early music:

"Quis, quid, ubi, quibus auxiliis, cur, quomodo, quando?"
                                              (Tertullian)
(Translates as "Who, what, where, by what means, why, how, when?")

My chosen instrument for my exam was, however, the piano, and I occasionally went to Hampstead for my lessons with Harold Craxton, with whom I studied for seven years from the age of sixteen. With him I prepared a 40-minute programme from memory. This included Bach's Chromatic Fantasy and Fugue, a Chopin Nocturne, and Ravel's Sonatine. The exam was held in St John's, and I remember the external examiner was Sir Ernest Bullock from the RCM, and two others. After my recital, I was put through a taxing series of practical tests. These included Score Reading a choral piece with baritone and C clefs – about five staves, only one of which was in an easily recognisable clef; playing some figured bass; improvising freely on a theme I think George Guest had composed; sight-reading an orchestral score; and finally a test I have always found difficult because of my perfect pitch: a very complicated, chromatic piece to transpose.

I did, however, get a Star for this section, so honour was satisfied, and Philip Radcliffe sent me a sweet card (which I kept)
to say he'd just been up to the Senate House, and seen on the
Board that I'd become a Batchelor!

Nigel's red MG –
CLU 815, 1958

Fred, Thelma
and Elizabeth,
Henley, 1958

Thurston Dart,
1959, last supervision
before Mus. B.

Vivian Trower with Brumas, 1959

Sally and Michael Werry, 1961

June 3rd 1961, Whitehall Court

Pond House, Dulwich Village, 1962–1969

RJW CBE, 1965

Attending a wedding at
St James's Piccadilly, 1969

Jane, Mary, James and
John with Janette Dodd,
Malta, 1969

With Margo at
Belair, 1970

Vanessa and Brian Doe, 1970

In the garden at Alleyn Rd, 1973

Redhead stars in baroque music recital

Cambridge Evening News 12.3.76

English Taskin Players, Girton College, Chapel, reviewed by JAMES DAY.

GENTLEMEN p r e f e r blondes, perhaps; but I'll settle for charming redheads, at any rate as exemplified by Elizabeth Werry.

Together with Peter Lloyd, they represented the English Taskin Players in a short but attractive recital or baroque music in Girton College Chapel yesterday evening.

The English Taskin Players are a high-powered group of chamber musicians who have won their musical spurs in such orchestras as the LSO, the ECO and the LPO; and Elizabeth Werry (no stranger to her old college) is their continuo player. Lucky them.

The concert was notable not only for Miss Werry's adroit fingerwork and choice of clear bright registration, but for Mr. Lloyd's full, substantial tone and excellent sense of both line and implied counterpoint in the flute parts. Thias was particularly notable in his solo contribution: J. S. Bach's A minor Partita, where the picking out of the various parts in the Allemande and the limpid richness of the Sarabande were particularly fine.

Miss Werry performed Handel's F major Suite with neat ornamentation and appealingly wayward rhythm in the slower movements; she built up the final Allegro with pointed, springy movement, and played Bach's G major Fantasia with a brilliantly fluent opening and nicely ebbing and flowing middle section.

Together, they formed a well-integrated and balanced team in the opening Handel F major Sonata and in the closing work—Bach's G minor flute Sonata, a most satisfying performance, particularly in the mobile Adagio.

Elinor and James, 1980

Recital at West Rd Concert Hall Cambridge 1979

English Taskin Players concert at Wigmore Hall, March 1980:
Roger Birnstingl, Elizabeth, Peter Lloyd, Neil Black

English Taskin Players (Law Society, 1980): Carmel Kaine,
Elizabeth, Charles Tunnell, Neil Black

Jane's last
term at King's
Canterbury,
1981

King's Choristers,
Christmas 1981

Hilly Beaufort with
Fleur and Bess,
1998

Foundlings Concert 2006, Elizabeth with Martin Prendergast
and Alan Rusbridger

The whole family, May 2011, Dulwich Picture Gallery

Dulwich

On leaving Cambridge I lived in a bed-sit in Chelsea (16 Sydney Street) and began to do Young Artists' Recitals for the ISM (Wigmore Hall), play for the Park Lane Group at 4 St James' Square, work as a freelance accompanist for small operatic groups, and accept as much work as I could get playing for singers and instrumentalists. I also began some teaching part-time, at the Oratory School in Chelsea, at Putney High School, and Datchelor. I accepted a post as Organist at St Mark's Regent's Park (the Zoo church), and occasionally sang in a double quartet with Nigel at St Clement Danes'. Noelle Barker was a soprano in this group. One evening I went to see the famous accompanist, Gerald Moore, whom I so much admired. Quite a daunting visit: he asked me to transpose something from "Dichterliebe" at sight. If I didn't already know it, I began to realise that to be a really good musician you need to have nerves of steel.

Born July 4th 1933, Nigel was an only child, and had rather a solitary boyhood surrounded by adults. His father, Fred, was born in 1900 in the North Riding of Yorkshire, the second of four children – William, Frederick, Amy and Charles. Their father, Arthur, was foreman of a local quarry. Their mother was Evelyn Maud Graham Jackson, from the village of Great Ayton.

Fred attended Sir William Turner's Grammar School in Redcar, where he was Head Boy. He won an Exhibition to Pembroke College in 1917, and was reading History until his eighteenth birthday (10th April 1918) when he was called up by the Durham Light Infantry and spent six months in the trenches before the war ended and he was able to return to Cambridge.

The family in Redcar was not well off (Fred had regularly sent his army pay home), and he was determined to make good in his chosen profession, the Law. His elder brother, William, was educated at Dulwich College, by the uncle who had founded the family firm (Rowe and Maw) in the 1880s. This uncle is remembered for a little book he wrote on the Bread Riots of the 1880s.

After graduating, Fred was articled to his uncle, and lived with the family in Streatham. He told me that he lived on a pittance during those years, and he kept meticulous accounts of his out-goings, spending very little on food (1½d for a bun for lunch), saving the tram fare by walking home. He did not get on with his uncle, clearly resenting the fact that he had not had his brother's education. (William had returned to the North and became a surveyor; he subsequently married and had a son and a daughter – John and Mary – but we did not know them.)

When Fred qualified as a Solicitor, he chose not to stay in the firm, but accepted a job with Fry's of Bristol. However, in 1927 his uncle died suddenly, and Fred became Senior Partner of Rowe and Maw at the age of 27. He was an outstanding lawyer, and the firm flourished.

In 1932 he married Thelma Valentine Crisp, the fourth daugh-ter of a Courage's Brewery Manager. The four girls were

Sheila, Ailsa, Lorna and Thelma. Thelma was an attractive
dancer whom Fred had met at St Luke's Church, West Norwood.
She loved children, but found producing one of her own and
caring for him very hard, despite having help. Fred and Thelma
moved to Alleyn Park early in their married life, and one of
Nigel's earliest memories was of being woken up to see the
Crystal Palace burning in the Autumn of 1936 when he was
three-and-a-half.

Fred's practice became more and more successful, and his
important clients included Ted Lewis (an old friend from
Trinity, later Sir Edward Lewis, Chairman of Decca) and
Sir Jules Thorn (of Thorn Electrical). He also acted for the
American Government.

As a small boy Nigel attended Dulwich Prep, down the road
from their house, until the war years necessitated their spending time in Abinger, Surrey, to avoid the Blitz. But the to-ing and
fro-ing took a toll on them all. Fred stayed in Dulwich, joining
the Home Guard but also working at the office. Thelma obviously found these years difficult and began to drink heavily.

Nigel went to board at Westminster as things were unsatis-
factory at home, and by the time we met, it was apparent
that he had had little family life such as we had enjoyed. No
brothers or sisters, no dog, not even a cat. He had one cousin,
Wendy Allingham (Lorna's daughter) who lived in Streatham.
The only other cousin he saw something of was Pamela Jury
(Amy's daughter), but they lived in Scotland. So, sadly, it was
a lonely childhood.

He loved singing in the Church Choir at St Stephen's, Dulwich,
together with his father, and as a boy treble he had made a

record for Decca, on which he sang "Who is Sylvia?" (Schubert), and then, with his father, a touching little Victorian duet, "My True Love hath my Heart".

National Service must have been a wonderful opportunity for Nigel. He joined the Royal West Kents, and was with Peter Morley-Jacob (a schoolfriend) and Mike Nyren. But he was not given the chance to serve in Malaya or Egypt as many of his contemporaries were. Instead he stayed at the Brigade HQ in Tonbridge for the whole of his two years, despite his commission.

Princess Marina was the Patron of the Royal West Kents, and I remember a couple of splendid Regimental Balls when she was present. These were grand affairs, with the men wearing their Reds, and all of us girls wearing long white gloves in the presence of royalty. One of these Balls was held in a hotel in Knightsbridge, one I think in Tonbridge somewhere.

Then there would be the Boat Race Ball, held at the Dorchester, especially enjoyable if Cambridge had won – which I think we mostly did in those years. We had tremendous fun going to the Races at Henley too (into the Phyllis Court enclosure, usually), and also going to Glyndebourne with a party of old Cambridge friends. The soprano Rae Woodland, a friend of Martin Briggs, had been taken up by Sir Thomas Beecham, and had a small part in whatever we were seeing that evening, probably 1958. Was it "The Magic Flute"? I can't now remember. Because it was raining so hard, the picnic in the Organ Room is my clearest memory of that evening.

But many more performances were to follow, and those bright years were filled with happy events and memories. We got engaged at Glyndebourne, and decided to get married the day after Solicitors' Finals results came out, which was to be June 1961. Sadly, Nigel's mother Thelma died in March 1960, of an alcohol-related illness, aged only 53.

Twice, around this time, Nigel joined us for family holidays abroad, once in Austria where we were staying on Bodensee. We found in a tiny chapel at Ossiachersee an interesting old Baroque organ with a painted screen depicting St Cecilia in all her glory. The pedal board was extraordinary – only about five or six notes as I remember, but certainly bottom C, F, G and C. We took some pictures, and I wrote an article for "The Musical Times" on our return. Dreadful horse-flies on that lake – we didn't want to go back there.

Another time we were in Mallorca at Puerto d'Andraitz, and Nigel joined us for a week. He was still doing his Articles, and Diana was doing six months at a TB hospital at Midhurst, Sussex. She had a tubercular ulcer which needed treatment while we were there, and this meant visiting a local GP. Here, Ping's competent Spanish was a great asset. Wherever we travelled she turned her mind towards learning a new language. Greek came soon after this trip. She really was such an example to all of us – her energy was prodigious and her enthusiasm and optimism infectious.

We all owed so much to her. She gave us the stability to cope with whatever life would throw at us, and from our earliest years we were encouraged to be both tolerant of others but self-critical. When Diana was about eight she expressed an interest in becoming a nurse, and remembers Ping saying, "Do you want to empty bed-pans all day? Why not be a doctor? …" The seed was sown, and Diana became a Consultant Radiologist.

After being so self-reliant during our seven years in Canada, it might have been easy for Ping to take a back seat in the family, for when we returned to bleak Lancashire and, soon after, to cold Yorkshire, she had no job. But it was her quiet conviction that we could all do better in the South that carried us through those tough four years. She took a job teaching French and Latin at "The Towers" in Saltburn (a little private school for "nice girls"), enabling Diana and me to have all those piano lessons. And it was her persistence and salary that led to us going abroad for those lovely long holidays, year after year while we were still at school. The habits of practice, homework, exercising the dog and helping with the household chores were ingrained in us thanks to her, and it was her strong hand in a velvet glove that helped shape my father's career in the world of education.

She it was who encouraged him to apply for a Headship in London – Kingsley Secondary Modern School in Chelsea in 1952. Then in 1957 he was appointed to the Headship of Tollington Park School in Islington. This large new Comprehensive was the amalgamation of three existing schools, with a purpose-built new block. The school had around 1800 pupils, boys and girls, and there were at least twelve different nationalities represented. It would be untrue to say the school had no problems. This was the time of the Greek Cypriot and Turkish unrest, and there were also many West Indian children who were members of gangs. But my father was a strong disciplinarian, and was well-liked and respected. After about eight years in the job, the School had a General Inspection and received a glowing report. In the Queen's Birthday Honours List of 1965, he was awarded the CBE for Services to Education. He was also a member of the National Libraries Committee, sat on the Board of the Brain Committee for Drug Addiction, and in retirement he chaired the Civil Service Commission Board. It was entirely typical of him that after the ceremony at Buckingham Palace with us in tow, followed by a celebration lunch at "The White Tower", he went straight back to school, got the children all together in the Hall to show them his CBE, saying, "The Queen has given me this medal for all of you." No wonder he still had twenty-five of his original members of staff when he retired in 1970.

Nigel and I married at St Olave's Church, Hart Street, in the City. This, the Datchelor church we knew so well, was a most romantic setting – the Pepys church, where we had often sung at school for the Clothworkers. The Dean of Pembroke married us, the music was provided by our friends from King's (including Purcell's "My Beloved Spake") and the organist was Gerald Hendrie (Selwyn). Diana and Vanessa were my bridesmaids, and as it was sunny, the reception was lovely on the terrace at Whitehall Court.

We lived for a year or so in a mansion flat in W1 (27 Cumberland Mansions), but just before Jane was born we heard of a large house in Dulwich. The Dulwich College Estate Governors were wanting to develop the seven acres of Pond Meadow, and the Chairman of the Governors (none other than FGM) encouraged us to take a lease on this old property, Pond House, built in 1756, with Victorian additions.

And so began our long association with Dulwich. Nan and her husband Bert Horsey moved with us, and were our faithful retainers for many years, an absolutely invaluable help during those early years when the children were small. I had first met Nan when I was living in Mrs Battley's house in Chelsea. Nan, the eldest of a very large Scots family, was brought up by her grandmother in the tiny village of Aberchirder by Huntley, 40 miles from Aberdeen. When she left school, she went to work as a kitchen maid in the Devonshire's London house in Belgrave

Square, and would move with the staff to their other proper-
ties around the country at different times of year. She told me
that her ambition had been to become a lady's maid, but this
never happened, possibly because of her limited education.
More likely it was her meetings on the back steps in Belgravia
with Bert, the maintenance man from Daimler's who came to
look after the car. Anyway, she married him before the war,
and it was our luck that when she first saw Jane ("Oh, the little
sweetling!") she never looked back.

It was Nan who taught me how to run a large house, and
nothing ever fazed her. If it were silver-cleaning day and there
was a family crisis suddenly, she took charge, and Pond House
ran like clockwork thanks to her. We had seven very happy
years there, during which, to my great delight and constant
joy, Jane and Mary, James and John made their appearance,
in 1962, 1964, 1966 and 1968. Janette Dodd moved in to help
when James arrived, and we had also by then acquired a couple
of Labradors and two kittens (Russian blues from the Vlasto
household in Cambridge).

A few months before we married, Nigel very generously gave
me a Steinway grand which we watched being reconditioned by
Bob Glazebrook in the old Hanover Square workshops. Over the
years that followed, Bob never failed to care for my instrument,
even when he rose to be Managing Director. He was a constant
friend and a brilliant technician.

I began to build up my teaching from home, and knew this was
my metier. The centre of my life has always been the family,
and to be able to work at home with the children all around
was ideal. We made a lot of friends as soon as we settled in
the Village, and my violinist schoolfriend Elizabeth's husband

Wyndham Lloyd-Davies became a close friend of Nigel. He had been at Rugby with the oboist Neil Black, and I began to work with Neil and other players in the London orchestras, and their children sometimes became my pupils.

One of our most devoted and close friends was "Happy" (Eve Happell), a near neighbour in Village Way. She loved us all, was a wonderful friend and always there when needed most. I remember a power cut, Pond House in absolute darkness, and four small children in the bath. Exciting maybe, but scary; and suddenly there was Happy at the door with a pile of candles. She sometimes came on holiday with us, and helped me cope with any problems, large or small. All this with an invalid husband too.

Fanny and Bob Alexander were among our lawyer friends at this time, and Fanny (later Burton) became a very good friend in later years.

Other close Dulwich friends were Camilla and Peter Wykes, and Hilly Beaufort, whose son Myles was John's best friend. The girls started nursery school and began to make friends locally too. Life became busier and I was lucky to have so much help. Nigel began to take on large cases, often of big company takeovers, and he acted for the American government in some very high-profile cases, including James Earl Ray, Jack Ruby, Dandy Kim and Caborn Waterfield. He began to find the pressure of family life overwhelming, and in 1972 he was found to have renal TB, necessitating a nefrectomy, from which it took him a long time to recover. We divorced in May 1974.

When the children were young, one of our favourite places was Malta, and for several years we rented a house in the village of Attard, where our next-door neighbours, Miriam and Joe Cutajar, became my very good friends. We drove all over the island, finding different beaches, and got to know Paradise Bay and Medina (remember the ramparts of the Xara Palace Hotel?) and the beautiful little island of Comino.

The Cutajars were always ready to help when things went wrong, when we needed a doctor from Valleta to see baby John, a few months old, who had picked up a nasty bug they called "Malta dog tummy". Joe fixed the loo when it packed up, told me how to get rid of maggots in my cheese cupboard, and cockroaches under the steps. He it was, too, who fielded the long-distance phone call on 16th August 1968 from Diana in England. She gave us the tragic news that our only brother John had died suddenly and unexpectedly of natural causes at the age of 36, leaving his son Michael and daughter Sally, then aged thirteen and ten.

This was the greatest sadness our family has had to bear: Ping never quite came to terms with the loss of her only son. As the years go by, we are all encouraged by events to enjoy today.

On several of our summer trips, Nanny and Nampa came abroad with us. Apart from Malta, we visited the island of Poros with them, and had a scary time nearly missing the ferry back to Piraeus due to a typical Greek mix-up over the tickets – but saved at the eleventh hour by the Headmaster buttonholing the Captain on the quayside. We also visited Spain and Mallorca a couple of times, once meeting Mary Foulds and her son David (then fourteen and just the right age for Jane) in Paguera. We have remained good friends over the years.

The children all attended the Dulwich schools: first the Prep, then Jane and Mary went to James Allen's Girls' School until they chose, at the ages of fourteen and eleven, to go to Mary Datchelor Girls' School in Camberwell, which was due to close before their sixth form years. Through the local schools, I met and became very good friends with Pamela Mann and Thelma Van Til, and also got to know a distinguished Norwegian lady, Gunvor Stallybrass (widow of E.M. Forster's editor, Oliver) who allowed me to use her large Victorian studio on Sydenham Hill for many Pupils' Concerts over the years. One evening, after playing in a Duet Recital in Dulwich Gallery, a member of the audience turned out to be Jacqueline Gilbert (Leveaux), a friend from my schooldays, whose mother had taught French at Kingsley School. Both Jackie and Pam remember their schools being evacuated during the war – Jackie at the Lycée went to a hotel in Ullswater, and Pam remembers sleeping in an icy-cold dormitory at Chatsworth, beneath a magnificent Van Eyck.

Jane's bosom friend for many years was Sara Skinner, whose father was a local GP. Sara later became Head of Music at Rosemead Prep. Mary's best friend was a sweet girl, Brigitte Rhodes, who tragically took her own life at the age of 29. James' and John's close friendship with the Francis twins, James and David, survived decades. Our life was quiet and uneventful, apart from occasional cheap holidays abroad.

By this time the children and I had moved to a roomy Victorian house (18 Alleyn Road), with seven bedrooms, five cellars, and a 200ft garden – a great house for a growing family and for one yellow Labrador, Margo. She had three litters, and the puppies were all over Dulwich. One litter was called after Harpsichords. Margo's successors were Honey (quite the best), Bess, and Amber. In her later years, Amber went to live with my god-son, Christopher Fisher-Dodd, on the family farm in Somerset.

Chris cared for her devotedly, and occasionally I took Amber walking over the moors in Devon.

For a couple of years in the 1970s, we had two Australian musicians living with us while they were studying in London – first Christine Harriott (soprano), and then her friend Deidre Rickards (a pianist). We loved having them, and they came back over the years to visit us.

James went to Dulwich College at the age of nine and, soon after, John became a chorister at King's College Cambridge. All the children played two instruments: Jane flute, Mary 'cello, James bassoon and John violin, and they all played the piano as well. Our music room was large enough to hold concerts, which we did regularly, and by the time Jane was about fifteen, she had a few little flute pupils too. In those days there were no activities after school, apart from Brownies, swimming lessons at Crystal Palace, or dancing classes with Gabrielle Armstrong. No mobile phones and very little TV, so looking back our lives did seem peaceful.

There was time for croquet in the garden, walks in Dulwich woods, 'cello lessons in Foot's Cray with Margaret Napier and violin lessons in Beckenham with Martin Jones. Cousins were too far away: John's children at boarding school in North Yorkshire and Diana's daughter, seven years younger than John, so really a different generation. So the Graham-Maw children grew up like a little army, very close to each other. Occasionally, foreign exchange visitors came to stay, or choristers during the holidays.

Dulwich has always been a lovely place to live, with its little street of old shops, the infants' and the junior schools and many large old houses and gardens. At the heart of the village is the College Chapel (Christ's Chapel of God's Gift) where Jane, Mary and James were confirmed. With its alms-houses, the chapel is next door to the Picture Gallery, where so many cultural events take place: concerts, lectures and special exhibitions in addition to the permanent collection of Old Masters. All the local schools use the Gallery (James studied History of Art there with Giles Waterfield).

The gardens are used in the summer for amateur Shakespeare performances, and I remember picnics on the grass with old friends Drs Margaret (Whichelow) and Brian Cox, visiting from Linton. Many times the Gallery proved a wonderful meeting place for long-time pals, Judith Rodden from Saffron Walden, Ruth Fletcher from Beverley, among many others – not forgetting my Australian friends. I remember again and again my Granny's advice: "Those friends thou hast …".

From Alleyn Road on Sundays we would often drive out to Cuffley, Hertfordshire, to have a super Sunday lunch with my parents (now known as Nanny and Nampa), then walk the dogs in Cuffley Woods, and return to the house for a large tea before driving home again. Or we would call on Grandfather at 21 Alleyn Park after morning service at St Stephen's, and have orange juice and twiglets with him and his second wife, Betty.

We saw little of the Werry cousins until Sally went to Goldsmiths' College to read music. She subsequently became a successful flute teacher in Guildford. Michael became an engineer and worked abroad.

As the children grew older, I had more time to devote to my teaching and playing, and in the 1970s, our chamber group, The English Taskin Players, was formed. I remember Ping

encouraging Diana and me to choose a career which could
fit around a family life (assuming that we did want one). The
obvious choice for me, coming from a teaching background,
was to pursue the kind of life I have in fact enjoyed. I used to
teach most days for three hours or so after school, and most of
Saturday. The influence of Ella, my wonderful teacher when
I was at such an impressionable age (twelve to sixteen), has
inspired all my work as an adult musician. Ella worked pas-
sionately until she dropped, and I imagine I shall do the same.
Apparently I knew when I was eight what I wanted to do.

I have been fortunate to work in an area where young people
are enthusiastic, ambitious and gifted, and also are surrounded
by supportive parents. Over a good many years I have taught
around 350 pupils of all ages and abilities, the youngest being
five or so, the oldest over 80. The vast majority have become
the world's listeners, playing for themselves for pleasure.

A handful have become professional musicians, and among
those, I remember Paul Brough (conductor), Sara Skinner
(pianist and singer), Huw Williams (organist), Julia Palmer
(pianist and 'cellist), Sophie Cotton (composer), Jane Werry
(conductor), Alex Stobbs (pianist). But a far greater number
have excelled in other walks of life (medicine, law and so on)
for whom music has become an absorbing interest, hobby
and relaxation. Among many others, I remember particularly Carine Powell (Dr), Nicholas Coombs (diplomat), Katie
Haylock (teacher), Helen Leach (barrister), Lucy Cary-Elwes
(financier), Alice King-Farlow (Education, National Theatre),
Michiko Matthews (librarian) and Sean Lloyd (engineer).

It was in the 1970s, too, that I bought a lovely harpsichord made
by William Dowd, a copy of a 1760 Taskin instrument, and spent

ten days in Antwerp on a masterclass run by Kenneth Gilbert, the French-Canadian harpsichordist, in 1974.

We would sometimes holiday in Devon, too, keeping in touch with "Cousin" Susie (Hoskins) who, for many years, was librarian of Okehampton, a real Devonian and always a true friend. In that summer of 1974 we were holidaying with the Blacks at Sticklepath, near to Okehampton, and it was while we were blackberrying on Dartmoor one afternoon that the idea of forming a chamber group was born. Of course, Neil's favourite friends were invited to join, and the English Taskin Players group was founded with Peter Lloyd (flute), Neil Black (oboe), Roger Birnstingl (bassoon), Carmel Kaine (violin), Charles Tunnell ('cello) and myself (harpsichord). Our first recital on the South Bank, in March 1975, had a rave notice from Dominic Gill in the Financial Times, and we were off to a brilliant start. We played all over the country for the next twenty years or so, and it was a wonderful opportunity for me to play with such fine musicians. Occasionally we would invite other performers: Richard Adeney (flute), Janice Knight (oboe), Michael Chapman (bassoon), John Willison (violin), and David Strange ('cello). We were usually four players, and our repertoire was usually baroque music. We enjoyed so many memorable concerts at places such as York, Halifax, Folkestone, Aberystwyth, Rosehill, Sevenoaks, Bishopsbourne, Cambridge, Chatsworth, Windermere, Hayling Island, and of course, the Wigmore Hall and the Purcell Room – and Dulwich Picture Gallery! The Taskins flourished until the mid-90s; by then many younger groups had overtaken us – and the early music/ early instrument brigade marched in.

But playing with the English Taskin Players was the icing on the cake for me. My life in Dulwich was always centred around the family and its needs, and I had no difficulty in knowing what I wanted to do. Diana could have become a GP, but opted for the very demanding life of a consultant physician for which she was well-suited. Despite the demands of her various hospital posts (at Central Middlesex, Aberystwyth and finally at Basingstoke), she married Terry Lynch in 1972 and had a daughter Elinor (born 1975) who in 1994 married Simon Pope. They had two sons, Ben and Tom. Diana remained my closest friend of all. She married her second husband, John Edward Thomas, in 1982.

Through the 70s Nigel, always a keen sailor, introduced the children when they were quite young to the excitement of sailing in his yacht "Sparkling Spirit". They all enjoyed some adventurous holidays, crossing the Channel in less than perfect weather, and would regale me with stories of their exploits on their return. Often Nigel's old friend Ione Woollaston would accompany them, and I knew they'd be in safe hands and would wear their safety harnesses. Ione later married Nick Ashford, a naval man, and they settled happily in Alresford with many Labradors.

1977 was the year of the Queen's Silver Jubilee. Like many other roads in Dulwich, Alleyn Road had a street party, and many of the children who lived up and down the road formed an orchestra and marched up and down playing their instruments and wearing fancy dress. I do remember Peter Holmes (who lived opposite us) doing his best to organise the little band, but sadly he would conduct "Men of Harlech" in three time, which caused a certain amount of havoc. "LIZ RULES O.K." was chalked on several drives, including the Palmers', next door to us.

Then the girls joined the sixth form at King's, Canterbury, making wonderful friendships, among them Brett Wolstencroft,

Edmund de Waal, Clare Edwards, Sarah Marshall, Rob Weaver and Tom Phillips that I can remember. John left King's Choir as Head Chorister the year after he had visited Australia for a month. In January 1982 he went to Westminster School as a Music Scholar, to Grant's (Nigel's old House). Jane, after a term in a Swiss finishing school learning to ski expertly (and to walk down a staircase in a ball-gown without tripping), went off to Christ's as an Exhibitioner in English. The following year Mary joined the B.Ed course at Homerton for Music. James decided to study classical Japanese at Fitzwilliam. He married Elisabetta Pezzali in 1984, and bravely coped with little Arthur who was born in 1985 during James's gap year. John went to CCAT to study Music, ending up as a Bass in St John's College Choir.

In the early 1980s I moved to a smaller house in Peckarmans Wood, and bought a little student property in Cambridge (90 Sedgwick Street, off Mill Road). John lived there for a couple of years and went to the Guildhall to do a postgraduate Opera Diploma. I began to teach a few undergraduates (Huw Williams, organ scholar of Christ's who became Organist of St Paul's Cathedral) and the choristers at King's. Here I was able to guide some very gifted young players, the best of whom usually went on to Eton (and sometimes came back to King's as undergraduates). This was true of Alex Stobbs, who suffered from cystic fibrosis. Even as a nine-year-old he was an inspiration with his sunny outlook on life, but it was heart-breaking at the same time to witness his daily battle against ever-increasing odds. I donated the Elizabeth Werry Bach Prize, a silver trophy, to the Choir School in 2003.

I taught at King's for about ten years, and it was around this time that my adult pupils in London included Tam Mito (introduced to me by James, and later an economics professor in Kyoto), Angus McLachlan (architect from New Zealand), and Martin Prendergast, then the Commercial Arts Manager at the Guardian. Other interesting pupils were the distinguished barrister Harry Trusted, and his wife Mary Anderson, an economist.

About this time I was able to renew my contact with Girton, and a group of us, including Susan Curtis-Bennett, formed the London Girton Association, which soon went from strength to strength, with meetings and expeditions in the London area. I visited many excellent exhibitions at the British Museum with my dear friend Mary Roe – and also innumerable concerts. We set up the LGA Music Prize – £500, awarded annually to a gifted undergraduate at College, in exchange for a Recital at Eva Lomnicka's beautiful house in Queen Anne's Gate. Many Girtonian friends such as Monica Vincent (classicist turned 'cellist) would join us for these and other events at the National Portrait Gallery or the Royal Academy. I especially remember Julia Roskill, Margaret Goodrich and Gwen Loft coming from great distances to join us, as indeed did many others (like Barbara Dalling from Glasgow) who came to the Dulwich Picture Gallery where I volunteered on the Friends' Desk.

I had a connection with the Foundlings Museum, and regularly did lunchtime concerts there, with friends I could persuade to come and play, such as my clarinettist friend, Janet Eggleden. The Guardian had a Choir (organised by Martin Prendergast) and sometimes they put on a concert in a City church such as St James's Clerkenwell, and I would be the organist. Once we had a big event in the Art Gallery at the Foundlings, and we finished the programme with a Piano Threesome Galop de Concert, with Alan Rusbridger, Martin, and me in the middle.

I played in a number of other chamber groups at this time – a trio with Richard Gullan (violinist and a well-known neuro-surgeon) and Libby Wilde ('cello). For a couple of years I played in a Piano Duo with Timothy Barratt (Head of Keyboard at Dulwich College), and for about four years I was a member of the London Piano Quartet (later named Piano 40). This group, founded by Nadia Lasserson, played contemporary works for four pianists on two pianos, and most of these first-performances required lengthy hours of rehearsal time! We played in Oxford, at the Purcell Room, and at an EPTA conference in Budapest, among other venues.

Occasionally I played the organ when required at local churches, but ceased to have a regular post at St Mary le Strand when the Vicar (the Rev. Edward Thompson) retired. The demands of a family make a Sunday job almost impossible, as I had found years before when I briefly took on a job at St John's, Ladbroke Grove, before we moved to Dulwich. But playing for Datchelor Carols at St Olave's every December has been tremendous fun for years, with Mary Rose Seldon still conducting in her 80s.

In 1997 I formed a literary group, together with a few close friends, including Jean Cary-Elwes, Maggie Thomas, Elizabeth Fenwick, Barbara McFarlane, Claude Powell and Sheila Jones. This was most rewarding, and gave some direction to my haphazard reading. Although we lost a few members over the years, we became a very strong group, supporting each other through all manner of events, and incidentally reading a lot of unusual and fascinating books.

This all stood me in good stead when, some years later as a member of the Reform Club, I joined their long-established

Reading Group. This was a totally different experience from the all-ladies "Dulwich Literary Group", and intellectually was quite demanding. Most of the books and authors chosen I had never even heard of, let alone read. It was however very stimulating, and another opportunity to make new friends.

I have so much to be thankful for – my family, my friends, my pupils – I love them all – my home, my books and paintings and photograph albums, my dog, my garden, my walks in the woods and, of course, my music.

It gives me tremendous pleasure that my family are all around me, and that my children are all so happily married. I have two wonderful sons-in-law – Rupert Ross-Macdonald, married to Jane, and Paul Raikes, married to Mary; and two lovely daughters-in-law – Megan Slyfield, married to James, and Julia Smallbone, married to John. Between them, they have produced quite an array of children born between 1985 and 2010.

And so now to the next generation: my twelve beautiful grandchildren – Arthur, George, Holly, Thomas, Katy, Josie, Emily, Abby, Marnie, Rufus, Jago and Orpheus – all living nearby, happy and healthy and enjoying life to the full.

The future is yours.

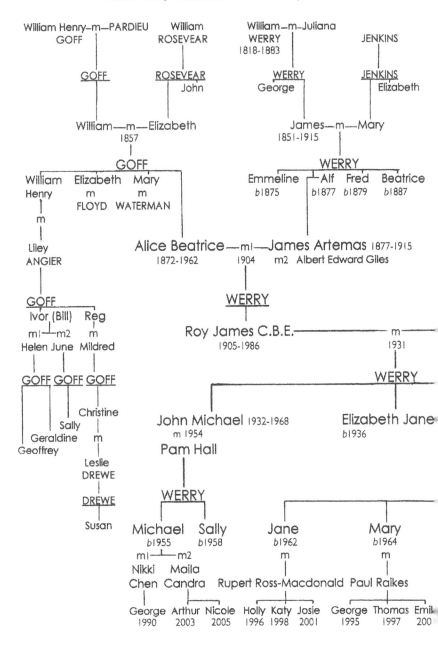

Thomas Werry b1656, Lanreath – Thomas Werry b1694 Duloe –
William Werry b1726, Duloe – William Werry b1756, St Austell

William Henry—m—PARDIEU
GOFF

William
ROSEVEAR

William—m—Juliana
WERRY
1818-1883

JENKINS

GOFF

ROSEVEAR
John

WERRY
George

JENKINS
Elizabeth

William—m—Elizabeth
1857

James—m—Mary
1851-1915

GOFF

William
Henry
m

Elizabeth
m
FLOYD

Mary
m
WATERMAN

WERRY

Emmeline
b1875

Alf
b1877

Fred
b1879

Beatrice
b1887

Liley
ANGIER

Alice Beatrice—m1—James Artemas 1877-1915
1872-1962   1904   m2 Albert Edward Giles

GOFF

Ivor (Bill)
m1—m2
Helen June

Reg
m
Mildred

WERRY

Roy James C.B.E.———————————m————
1905-1986   1931

GOFF   GOFF GOFF

Christine

Sally

WERRY

Geraldine
Geoffrey

m
Leslie
DREWE

John Michael 1932-1968
m 1954

Elizabeth Jane
b1936

Pam Hall

DREWE

Susan

WERRY

Michael
b1955
m1—m2
Nikki Maila
Chen Candra

Sally
b1958

Jane
b1962
m

Rupert Ross-Macdonald

Mary
b1964
m

Paul Raikes

George Arthur Nicole
1990   2003   2005

Holly Katy Josie
1996   1998 2001

George Thomas Emil
1995   1997   200

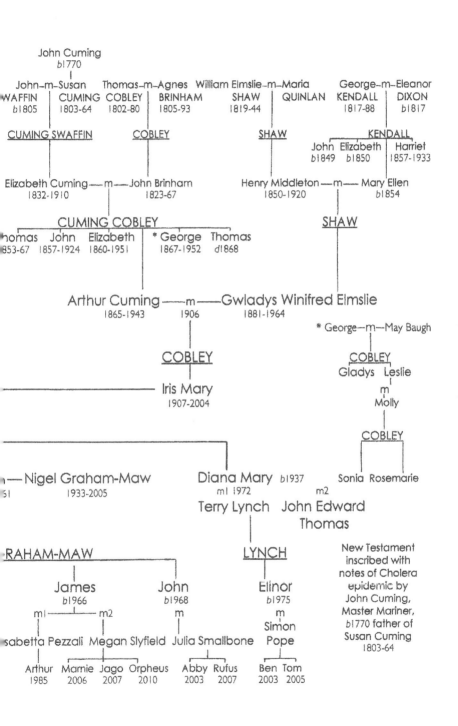

John Cuming
b1770

John—m—Susan   Thomas—m—Agnes   William Elmslie—m—Maria   George—m—Eleanor
WAFFIN | CUMING   COBLEY | BRINHAM   SHAW | QUINLAN   KENDALL | DIXON
b1805 | 1803-64   1802-80 | 1805-93   1819-44 | 1817-88 | b1817

CUMING SWAFFIN   COBLEY   SHAW   KENDALL
                                    John   Elizabeth | Harriet
                                    b1849   b1850 | 1857-1933

Elizabeth Cuming——m——John Brinham   Henry Middleton——m——Mary Ellen
1832-1910   1823-67   1850-1920   b1854

CUMING COBLEY   SHAW

Thomas   John   Elizabeth   * George   Thomas
1853-67   1857-1924 1860-1951   1867-1952   d1868

Arthur Cuming——m——Gwladys Winifred Elmslie
1865-1943   1906   1881-1964

COBLEY

                                    * George—m—May Baugh

                                    COBLEY
                                    Gladys   Leslie
                                             m
                                             Molly

Iris Mary
1907-2004

                                    COBLEY

———Nigel Graham-Maw   Diana Mary b1937   Sonia   Rosemarie
51   1933-2005   m1 1972   m2
                          Terry Lynch   John Edward
                                             Thomas

RAHAM-MAW   LYNCH   New Testament
                                                   inscribed with
   James   John   Elinor   notes of Cholera
   b1966   b1968   b1975   epidemic by
   m1——m2   m   m   John Cuming,
                           Simon   Master Mariner,
sabetta Pezzali Megan Slyfield Julia Smallbone Pope   b1770 father of
                                                   Susan Cuming
                                                   1803-64

Arthur Marnie Jago Orpheus   Abby Rufus   Ben   Tom
1985   2006   2007 2010   2003 2007   2003 2005

Acknowledgements

I would like to offer my thanks to those who have helped produce this little volume –

Wanda Whiteley for preparing and editing the text

John Barrett for help with the photographs

Walter M. Keesey (*Cambridge – A Sketch-book*, A.& C. Black Ltd) for the front cover illustration

My niece Sally Werry for researching Church and Public Records in search of the family history

Joanna Logan for co-ordinating the Family Tree

Jacqui Caulton my designer

And especially my daughter Jane for her support and encouragement throughout.

THE OLD COUNTRY

"Oh! The oak, and the ash,
And the bonny ivy tree –
They flourish at home in
My own country."